TEACHER RECOMMENDED

3RD GRADE COMMON CORE MATH
DAILY PRACTICE WORKBOOK

PART I: MULTIPLE CHOICE

ARGOPREP.COM

FREE ONLINE SYSTEM WITH VIDEO EXPLANATIONS

ArgoPrep is one of the leading providers of supplemental educational products and services. We offer affordable and effective test prep solutions to educators, parents and students. Learning should be fun and easy! For that reason, most of our workbooks come with detailed video answer explanations taught by one of our fabulous instructors.

Our goal is to make your life easier, so let us know how we can help you by e-mailing us at: info@argoprep.com.

ALL RIGHTS RESERVED
Copyright © 2022 by Argo Brothers, Inc.

ISBN: 978-1946755957
Published by Argo Brothers, Inc.

All rights reserved, no part of this book may be reproduced or distributed in any form or by any means without the written permission of Argo Brothers, Inc.
All the materials within are the exclusive property of Argo Brothers, Inc.

Acknowledgments:
Icons made by Freepik, Creaticca Creative Agency, Pixel perfect, Pixel Buddha, Smashicons, Twitter, Good Ware, Smalllikeart, Nikita Golubev, monkik, DinosoftLabs, Icon Pond from www.flaticon.com

ArgoPrep has won **over 10+ educational awards** for their workbooks and online learning platform. Here are a few highlighted awards!

TABLE OF CONTENTS

Foreward 10
Week 1 - *Place value & rounding* 12
Week 2 - *Adding & subtracting whole numbers up to 1,000* 19
Week 3 - *Multiplication* 25
Week 4 - *Multiplication & Division* 31
Week 5 - *Re-writing multiplication sentences as division and vice versa* 37
Week 6 - *Commutative, associative, and distributive properties* ... 43
Week 7 - *Real world word problems* 49
Week 8 - *Multi-step word problems* 55
Week 9 - *Fractions* 61
Week 10 - *Placing fractions on a number line* 67
Week 11 - *Comparing and ordering fractions* 73
Week 12 - *Telling time* 79
Week 13 - *Measurement* 85
Week 14 - *Bar graphs and pictographs* 91
Week 15 - *Measuring lengths & understanding line plots* 97
Week 16 - *Area* 103
Week 17 - *Real world word problems* 109
Week 18 - *Area and perimeter* 115
Week 19 - *Characteristics of shapes* 121
Week 20 - *Fractions and shapes* 127
End of Year Assessment 134
Answer Key 145

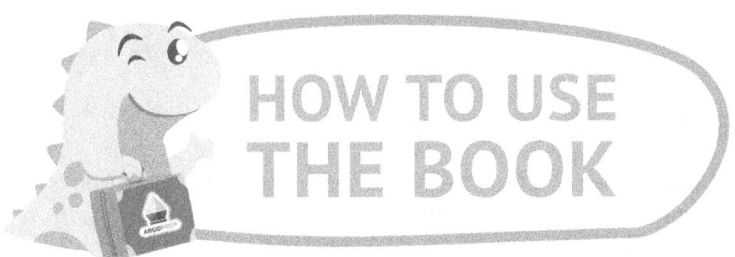

HOW TO USE THE BOOK

This workbook is designed to give lots of practice with the math Common Core State Standards (CCSS). By practicing and mastering this entire workbook, your child will become very familiar and comfortable with the state math exam. If you are a teacher using this workbook for your students, you will notice each question is labeled with the specific standard so you can easily assign your students problems in the workbook. This workbook takes the CCSS and divides them up among 20 weeks. By working on these problems on a daily basis, students will be able to (1) find any deficiencies in their understanding and/or practice of math and (2) have small successes each day that will build proficiency and confidence in their abilities.

We strongly recommend watching the videos as it will reinforce the fundamental concepts. Please note, scrap paper may be necessary while using this workbook so that the student has sufficient space to show their work.

For a detailed overview of the Common Core State Standards for 3rd grade, please visit: www.corestandards.org/Math/Content/3/introduction/

HOW TO WATCH VIDEO EXPLANATIONS
IT IS ABSOLUTELY FREE

Download our app:
ArgoPrep Video Explanations
to access videos on any mobile device or tablet.

or

Step 1 - Visit our website at: www.argoprep.com/k8
Step 2 - Click on the "Video Explanations" button located on the top right corner.
Step 3 - Choose the workbook you have and enjoy video explanations.

*You can scan this QR code to access **video explanations** as well.*

OTHER BOOKS BY ARGOPREP

Here are some other test prep workbooks by ArgoPrep you may be interested in. All of our workbooks come equipped with detailed video explanations to make your learning experience a breeze! Visit us at *www.argoprep.com*

COMMON CORE MATH SERIES

COMMON CORE ELA SERIES

INTRODUCING MATH!

Introducing Math! by ArgoPrep is an award-winning series created by certified teachers to provide students with high-quality practice problems. Our workbooks include topic overviews with instruction, practice questions, answer explanations along with digital access to video explanations. Practice in confidence - with ArgoPrep!

SCIENCE SERIES

Science Daily Practice Workbook by ArgoPrep is an award-winning series created by certified science teachers to help build mastery of foundational science skills. Our workbooks explore science topics in depth with ArgoPrep's 5 E'S to build science mastery.

KIDS SUMMER ACADEMY SERIES

ArgoPrep's Kids Summer Academy series helps prevent summer learning loss and gets students ready for their new school year by reinforcing core foundations in math, english and science. Our workbooks also introduce new concepts so students can get a head start and be on top of their game for the new school year!

WATER FIRE

MYSTICAL NINJA

GREEN POISON

FIRESTORM WARRIOR

RAPID NINJA

CAPTAIN ARGO

THUNDER WARRIOR

DANCE HERO

ADRASTOS THE SUPER WARRIOR

CAPTAIN BRAVERY

FOREWARD

Written by: Mary Miele, founder of The Evolved Education Company, K-12 licensed teacher in New York State and New York City, and author of Supporting School: A Guidebook for Parents and Educators, has spent the past twenty years working with students, educators and their families to improve their education experiences.

"By failing to prepare, you are preparing to fail."
- Benjamin Franklin

"Give me six hours to chop down a tree and I will spend the first four sharpening the axe."
Abraham Lincoln

Preparation is an essential, popular notion, which the most successful among us understand as necessary. **Argo Brothers** offers educators and students access to well-organized, user-friendly Common Core curriculum and test preparation materials in various mediums. Using the **Grade 3 Math Workbook: Common Core** allows us at **The Evolved Education Company** to utilize and implement the necessary curriculum so as to best prepare our students for mastery of Common Core modules and standardized state tests.

With the understanding that no one piece of curriculum can possibly serve every student, Argo Brothers has created an incredibly valuable resource for educators. The Grade 3 Math Workbook: Common Core follows the Common Core Standards and approaches problems from a variety of perspectives thereby ensuring students achieve a well-rounded understanding of the concepts being taught.

Considering the natural development of our children as well as the transparency needed around tests, standardized testing as an institution still has strides to make so as to appropriately support educators who work to help students prepare.

Parents can ensure education milestones are met by learning more about the Common Core Standards, purchasing the Argo Brothers books and by working together with whole child educators.

Additionally, parents of elementary and middle school children may consider the following tactics widely used by successful educators who help students to master the Common Core Standards using such books as this one:

1. Use the Evolved Education Paradigm to assess where your child is beginning his or her preparation. The paradigm accounts for one's academic history, learning style, school and family environment and social-emotional-physical-academic quotient. Please find more information about this paradigm and its benefits at *www.evolveded.com*.

2. Plan an appropriate long-term, study-time program. Children require time, repetition and practice to learn and master new material. Standardized tests require students have a deeply rooted mastery of topics, which cannot be achieved through cramming or one-dimensional review and practice.

3. Instruct, guide, practice and study. Students need to work through academic material in this sequence. First, they need to be taught how to approach the task or concept. Then, they need guidance as they acquire a new task or understanding of a new concept. Next, a student must practice independently and study the strategies and approaches over time. When students work through preparation in this sequence, they are well-prepared for tests.

4. Understand that standardized testing is an accepted form of assessment, emphasized in today's pre-kindergarten through college education experience. However, perspective is important. It is crucial to recognize that standardized tests present only one piece of the picture that represents your child's academic portfolio.

5. Always work closely with your child's educators to be sure the path you take in supporting your child is the best one possible, one that celebrates each child's strengths, talents and passions.

For more practice with 3rd Grade Math, be sure to check out our other book Common Core Math Workbook Grade 3: Free Response.

WEEK 1

VIDEO EXPLANATIONS — ARGOPREP.COM

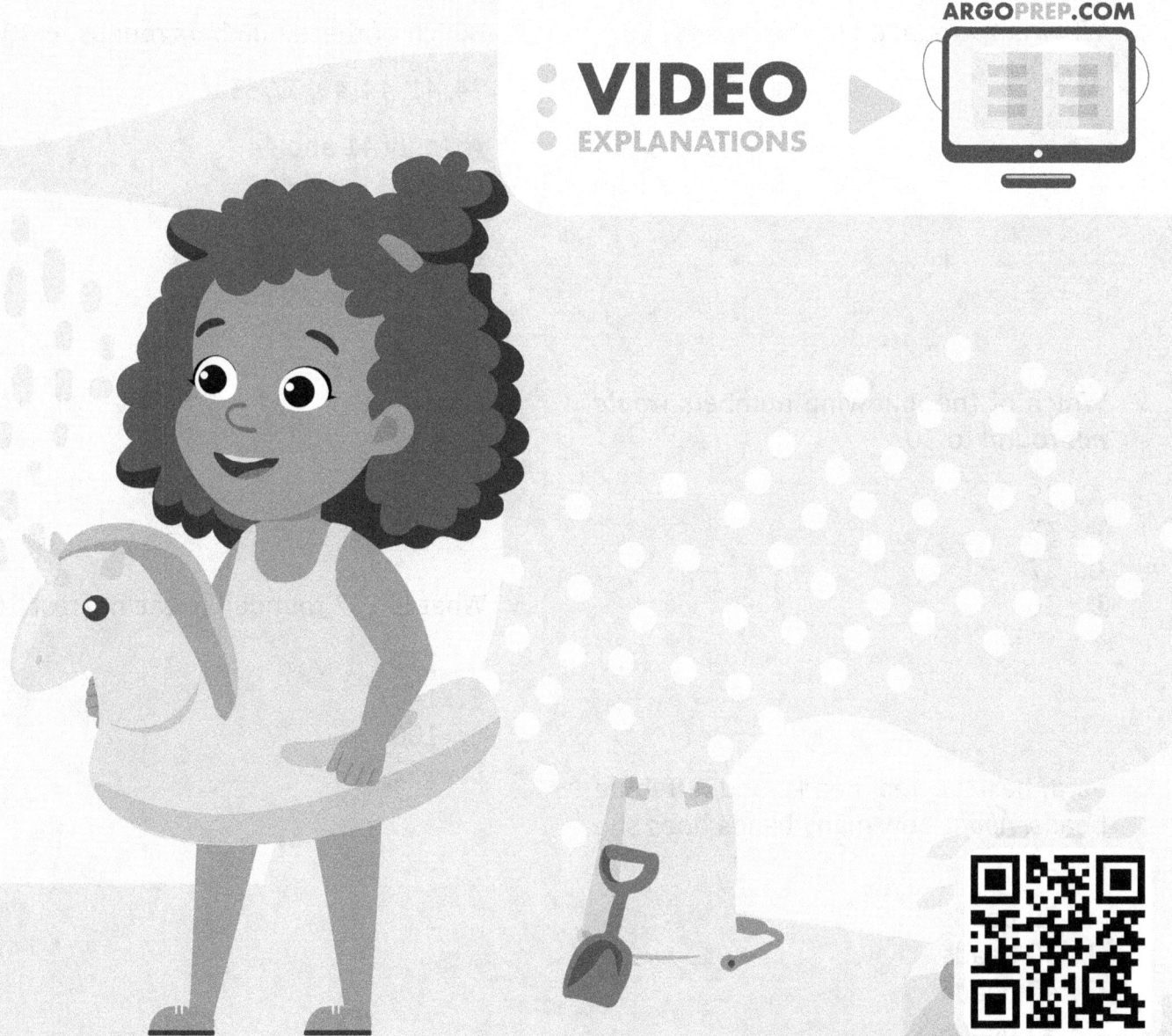

Week 1 is all about place value and rounding numbers. Rounding to the nearest 10 and nearest 100 will be the main focus, and will be useful in solving word problems and real-world situations that don't need exact amounts.

You can find detailed video explanations of each problem in the book by visiting: ArgoPrep.com

WEEK 1 : DAY 1

1. What is 19 rounded to the nearest 10?

    A. 10
    B. 20
    C. 19
    D. 30

    3.NBT.1

2. Which of the following numbers **would not** round to 30?

    A. 29
    B. 33
    C. 27
    D. 36

    3.NBT.1

3. Sara has 11 red beads and 28 blue beads. **About** how many beads does she have?

    A. 39 beads
    B. 30 beads
    C. 40 beads
    D. 45 beads

    3.NBT.1

4. Which of these numbers rounds to 40?

    24, 41, 44, 49, 37, 33

    A. only 41 and 44
    B. 41, 44 and 49
    C. only 37 and 41
    D. 37, 41, and 44

    3.NBT.1

5. What is 132 rounded to the nearest 10?

    A. 130
    B. 140
    C. 100
    D. 132

    3.NBT.1

TIP of the DAY

When rounding to the nearest ten, look at the ones digit. If the digit in the ones place value is 5 or greater, round up. If it's less than 5, round down!

WEEK 1 : DAY 2

1. Which of the following numbers rounds to 120 when rounding to the nearest 10?

   A. 109
   B. 112
   C. 119
   D. 129

   3.NBT.1

2. Jayce has 3 bags that each have 17 shells in them. *About* how many shells does she have?

   A. 51
   B. 30
   C. 50
   D. 60

   3.NBT.1

3. Which of the following numbers **will not** round to 300?

   A. 303
   B. 345
   C. 249
   D. 298

   3.NBT.1

4. Which of the following statements is *true*?

   A. 21 rounds down to 20
   B. 33 rounds up to 40
   C. 55 rounds down to 50
   D. 61 rounds up to 70

   3.NBT.1

5. Sandy needs to know how many shells are in her collection. She collected 49 today and 83 yesterday. *About* how many shells does she have, rounded to the nearest 10?

   A. 132
   B. 140
   C. 130
   D. 200

   3.NBT.1

6. What is 345 rounded to the nearest 100?

   A. 450
   B. 400
   C. 300
   D. 350

   3.NBT.1

TIP of the DAY

When solving word problems, always round first, then add or subtract. For example, if you have 3 groups of items, round all three groups first, then add the rounded amounts together!

15

WEEK 1 : DAY 3

1. What is 459 rounded to the nearest 100?

   A. 450
   B. 460
   C. 400
   D. 500

   3.NBT.1

2. Janell has 78 beads. She lost 27 beads. *About* how many beads does she have now?

   A. 51
   B. 50
   C. 80
   D. 30

   3.NBT.1

3. What is 159 rounded to the nearest 10 and the nearest 100?

   A. Nearest 10: 150; Nearest 100: 100
   B. Nearest 10: 160; Nearest 100: 100
   C. Nearest 10: 160; Nearest 100: 200
   D. Nearest 10: 150; Nearest 100: 200

   3.NBT.1

4. Which of the following statements is *false*?

   A. 56 would round up to 60
   B. 491 would round down to 400
   C. 183 would round up to 200
   D. 817 would round up to 820

   3.NBT.1

5. Which of the following numbers **would not** round to 300 if rounding to the nearest 100?

   A. 321
   B. 298
   C. 278
   D. 352

   3.NBT.1

6. What is 217 rounded to the nearest 10?

   A. 200
   B. 300
   C. 210
   D. 220

   3.NBT.1

TIP of the DAY

When rounding to the nearest 100, make sure to look at the digit in the tens place value. If it is 5 or more, round the number up to the next 100. If it is less than 5, round the number down to the previous 100.

WEEK 1 : DAY 4

1. What is 827 rounded to the nearest 100?

   A. 850
   B. 800
   C. 820
   D. 830

   3.NBT.1

2. Mr. Jackson has 345 pencils and 238 pens. **About** how many pens and pencils does he have altogether, rounded to the nearest 10?

   A. 590
   B. 500
   C. 600
   D. 583

   3.NBT.1

3. Which number would round to both 170 and 200?

   A. 167
   B. 179
   C. 175
   D. 164

   3.NBT.1

4. Which explanation shows how to round 234 to the nearest 100?

   A. Look at the ones digit, and round 234 to 300.
   B. Look at the ones digit, and round 234 to 230.
   C. Look at the tens digit, and round 234 to 200.
   D. Look at the tens digit, and round 234 to 300.

   3.NBT.1

5. What is 2,368 rounded to the nearest 100?

   A. 2,300
   B. 2,400
   C. 2,360
   D. 2,380

   3.NBT.1

6. What of the follow statements is *true*?

   A. 324 rounds to 330
   B. 324 rounds to 400
   C. 324 rounds to 350
   D. 324 rounds to 300

   3.NBT.1

When rounding, think about whether it would be best to round to the nearest 10 or to the nearest 100. Sometimes your answer makes more sense when rounding to one place value instead of another.

17

WEEK 1 : DAY 5

ASSESSMENT

1. What is 139 rounded to the nearest 10?

    A. 100
    B. 200
    C. 130
    D. 140

    3.NBT.1

2. Kellen needs to pick *all* the numbers that round to 200 when rounded to the nearest 100. Which numbers should he pick?

    192, 204, 154, 109, 231

    A. only 192 and 204
    B. only 192 and 109
    C. 192, 204, 154, and 231
    D. only 204 and 231

    3.NBT.1

3. Which number *does not* round to 80?

    A. 79
    B. 81
    C. 84
    D. 73

    3.NBT.1

4. Mr. Case has 27 students in his class, Mrs. Klein has 31, and Mrs. Jamison has 26. *About* how many students do they have altogether?

    A. 78 students
    B. 80 students
    C. 90 students
    D. 100 students

    3.NBT.1

5. There were 100 lollipops in the bag. 37 girls and 21 boys ate lollipops. *About* how many lollipops are left?

    A. 42
    B. 40
    C. 50
    D. 60

    3.NBT.1

6. Which of the following numbers rounds to 90 when rounded to the nearest 10?

    A. 84
    B. 92
    C. 109
    D. 97

    3.NBT.1

DAY 6
Challenge question

Chanel was adding together all the buttons in her collection. She had 227 in one box, 199 in another box, and 302 in her third box. *About* how many buttons did she have altogether, rounded to the nearest 100?

3.NBT.1

WEEK 2

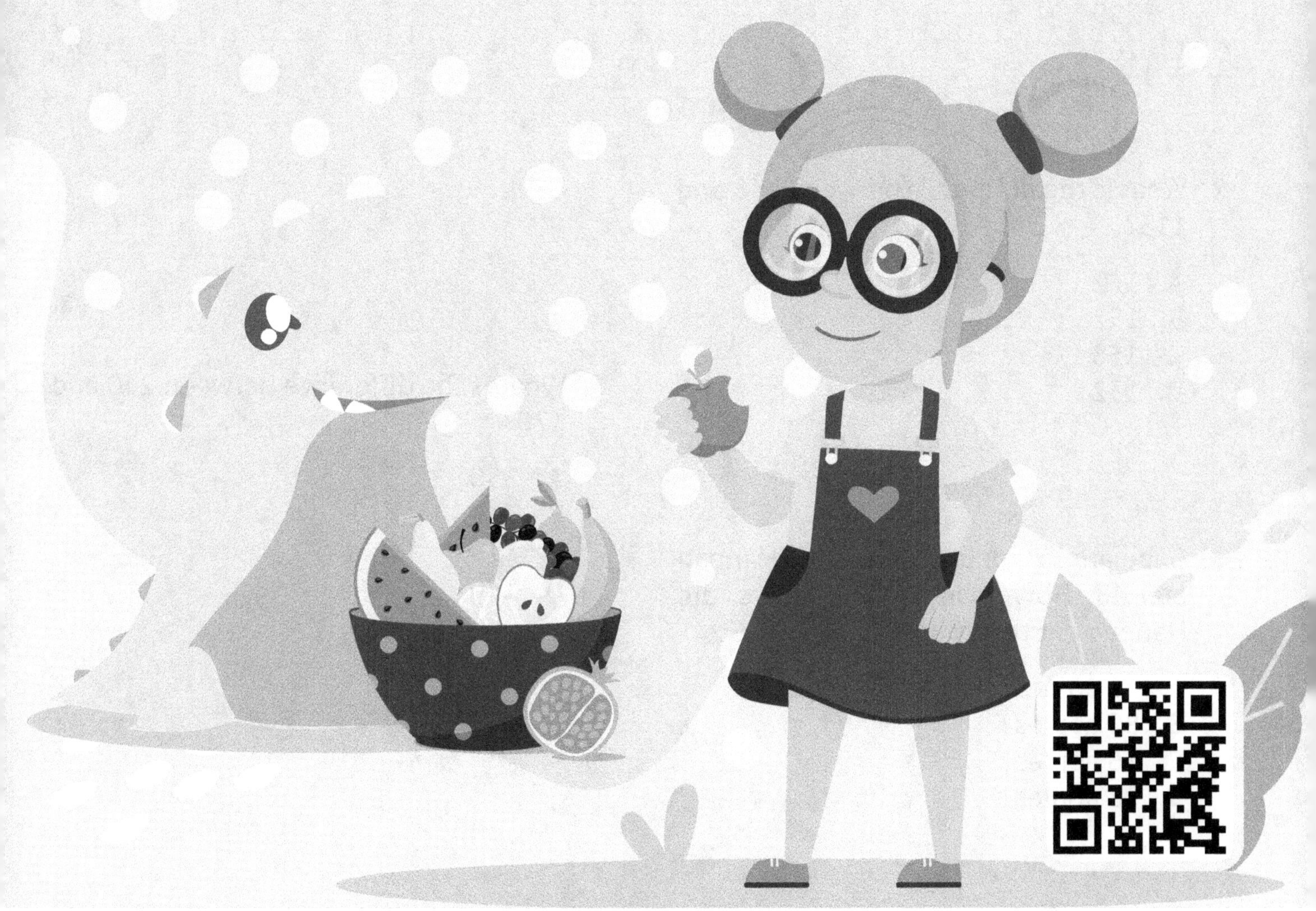

This week we are going to practice adding and subtracting whole numbers up to 1,000. You will "show what you know" when it comes to different properties of addition and subtraction, as well as using place value understanding to regroup.

You can find detailed video explanations of each problem in the book by visiting: ArgoPrep.com

WEEK 2 : DAY 1

1. The 3rd Grade has 137 students and the 4th Grade has 122 students. How many students are there in both grades altogether?

   A. 260
   B. 259
   C. 269
   D. 258

   3.NBT.2

2. What is the difference between 245 and 113?

   A. 122
   B. 152
   C. 158
   D. 132

   3.NBT.2

3. Gabe ate 32 apples this month. Hannah ate 48. How many more apples did Hannah eat than Gabe?

   A. 16 apples
   B. 80 apples
   C. 76 apples
   D. 18 apples

   3.NBT.2

4. What is the sum of 12, 23, and 44?

   A. 78
   B. 80
   C. 79
   D. 89

   3.NBT.2

5. What is the difference between 230 and 120?

   A. 350
   B. 340
   C. 110
   D. 120

   3.NBT.2

TIP of the DAY

When adding multiple numbers together, make sure you line up all digits in the correct place values! Put ones on top of ones, tens on top of tens, and hundred on top of hundreds.

WEEK 2 : DAY 2

1. What is the sum of 429 and 128?

   A. 556
   B. 557
   C. 548
   D. 547

   3.NBT.2

2. Carla has three boxes with 38 strawberries in each box. How many strawberries does Carla have in total?

   A. 76
   B. 66
   C. 104
   D. 114

   3.NBT.2

3. When adding 395 + 228, how many times do you need to regroup?

   A. You need to regroup three times when adding 395 + 228.
   B. You need to regroup twice when adding 395 + 228.
   C. You need to regroup once when adding 395 + 228.
   D. You do not need to regroup when adding 395 + 228.

   3.NBT.2

4. What is the sum of 609 + 327?

   A. 926
   B. 929
   C. 936
   D. 939

   3.NBT.2

5. Which addition sentence *does not* equal 1,000?

   A. 555 + 445
   B. 612 + 388
   C. 289 + 711
   D. 212 + 615

   3.NBT.2

6. Jessie has two pieces of string that are both 435 inches long. How long are the two pieces of string all together?

   A. 870 inches
   B. 435 inches
   C. 437 inches
   D. 860 inches

   3.NBT.2

TIP of the DAY

When regrouping in addition, make sure to remember that 10 ones make a new "ten", and 10 tens make a new "hundred".

WEEK 2 : DAY 3

1. What is the difference between 939 and 342?

   A. 617
   B. 1,281
   C. 697
   D. 597

   3.NBT.2

2. Joshua had 823 baseball cards. He sold 289 of them. How many does he have now?

   A. 666
   B. 534
   C. 536
   D. 1,112

   3.NBT.2

3. There are 689 daisies and 327 roses in the garden. *About* how many more daisies are there than roses, rounded to the nearest 100?

   A. 400
   B. 360
   C. 460
   D. 362

   3.NBT.1 / 3.NBT.2

4. Which equation does the number line most likely represent?

   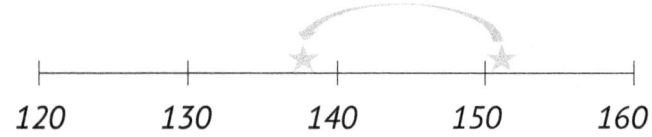

   A. 138 + 3 = 140
   B. 138 + 13 = 151
   C. 151 - 13 = 138
   D. 138 + 151 = 289

   3.NBT.2

5. Nancy started with 100 purses to sell. She sold 23 on Friday, 37 on Saturday, and 19 on Sunday. How many does she have left?

   A. 79 purses
   B. 21 purses
   C. 22 purses
   D. 20 purses

   3.NBT.2

TIP of the DAY

When regrouping in subtraction, make sure to go to the place value to the left to regroup. For example, if you need more tens to subtract, regroup by going to the hundreds place value.

WEEK 2 : DAY 4

1. Jaylen had 239 rocks. He lost 57 rocks, and then was given 112 rocks. How many rocks does he have now?

   A. 182 rocks
   B. 70 rocks
   C. 408 rocks
   D. 294 rocks

   3.NBT.2

2. What is the missing number in this equation?

   22 + ☐ = 47

   A. 25
   B. 26
   C. 69
   D. 20

   3.NBT.2

3. Yesterday, Catie had 38 eggs in her chicken coop. Today, there are 45 eggs. How many eggs did the chickens lay over night?

   A. 83 eggs
   B. 13 eggs
   C. 7 eggs
   D. 8 eggs

   3.NBT.2

4. Mr. Keil's class was selling tickets. If they want to sell 100 tickets total, how many more tickets do they need to sell?

Day	Tickets Sold
Monday	37
Tuesday	21
Wednesday	29

   A. 87 tickets
   B. 13 tickets
   C. 17 tickets
   D. 27 tickets

   3.NBT.2

5. What is the difference between 809 and 487?

   A. 482
   B. 1,296
   C. 322
   D. 222

   3.NBT.2

TIP of the DAY

You can switch the numbers of an addition sentence around to make a subtraction sentence. For example, if 14 + 16 = 30, then make a subtraction sentence that says 30 - 16 = 14, or 30 - 14 = 16. Addition and subtraction are called inverse operations.

WEEK 2 : DAY 5

ASSESSMENT

1. Which of the following statements is true about the equation below?

   714 - 569 = ?

   A. You need to regroup twice. The correct answer is 145.
   B. You need to regroup once. The correct answer is 265.
   C. You don't need to regroup. The correct answer is 255.
   D. You don't need to regroup. The correct answer is 282.

   3.NBT.2

2. What is the sum of 239, 123, and 449?

   A. 791
   B. 798
   C. 812
   D. 811

   3.NBT.2

3. Each class in the 3rd grade has 26 students. There are five 3rd grade classes. How many students are in the 3rd grade?

   A. 125 students
   B. 136 students
   C. 130 students
   D. 100 students

   3.NBT.2

4. What is the difference between 903 and 827?

   A. 86
   B. 76
   C. 34
   D. 24

   3.NBT.2

5. Gregory started his walk with 59 stones in his bag. At the end of his walk he had 72 stones. How many new stones did he collect while on his walk?

   A. 131 stones
   B. 27 stones
   C. 77 stones
   D. 13 stones

   3.NBT.2

6. Haley has 923 stickers in her collection. Janell only has 297 stickers. *About* how many more stickers does Haley have than Janell, rounded to the nearest 100?

   A. 620
   B. 626
   C. 600
   D. 630

   3.NBT.1

DAY 6
Challenge question

Find the sum of 343 and 459. Then subtract 219. What is your final answer?

3.NBT.2

24

WEEK 3

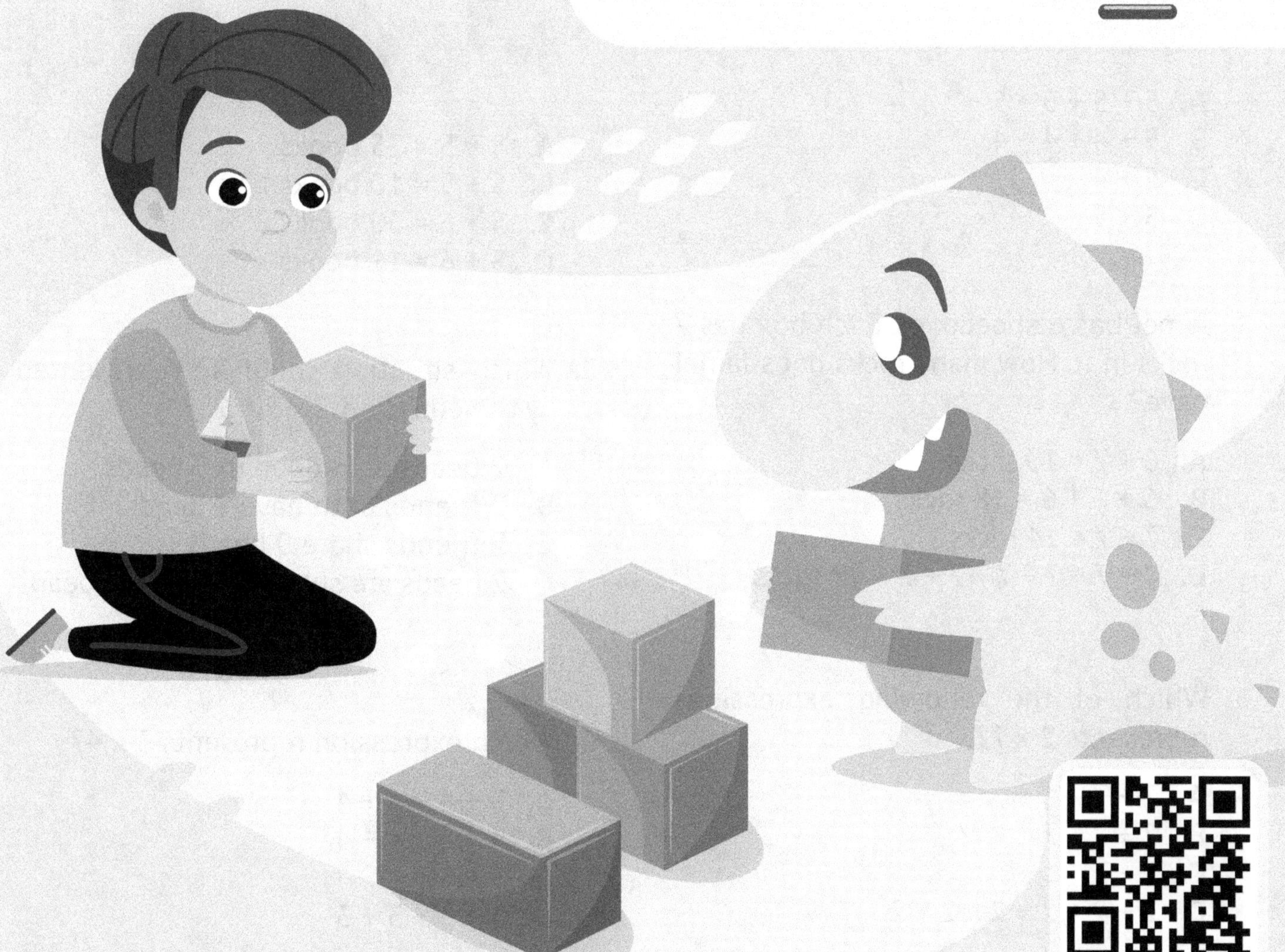

Week 3 is an exciting introduction to multiplication. You will have the chance to connect expressions and equations with equal group drawings and situations, as well as practicing multiplying by multiples of 10.

You can find detailed video explanations of each problem in the book by visiting: ArgoPrep.com

WEEK 3 : DAY 1

1. Which expression represents the number of stars below?

     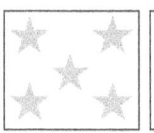 

   A. 5 + 5 + 5 + 5
   B. 5 + 4 + 4 + 4
   C. 5 + 4
   D. 5 + 5

   3.OA.1

2. Jamel has 6 shoeboxes. Each box has 7 rocks in it. How many rocks does Jamel have?

   A. 6 + 7 = 13 rocks
   B. 6 + 6 + 6 = 18 rocks
   C. 7 + 7 = 14 rocks
   D. 7 + 7 + 7 + 7 + 7 + 7 = 42 rocks

   3.OA.1

3. Which of the following expressions represents 2 x 7?

   A. 2 + 7
   B. 2 + 7 + 7
   C. 7 + 7
   D. 2 + 2 + 2 + 2 + 2 + 2

   3.OA.1

4. If Justin puts 5 books in each of the boxes below, which equation represents how many books he will have?

   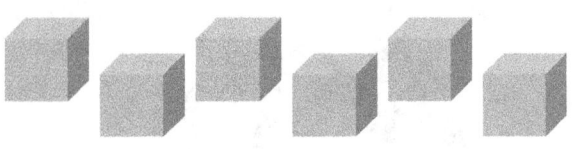

   A. 5 × 5 = 25 books
   B. 5 + 5 = 10 books
   C. 5 × 6 = 30 books
   D. 5 + 6 = 11 books

   3.OA.1

5. Which situation could be represented by the equation 2 x 9 = 18?

   A. 2 beads are added to 9 beads
   B. 2 friends both have 9 beads
   C. 2 friends share 9 beads
   D. 2 beads are subtracted from 9 beads

   3.OA.1

6. Which expression represents 3 x 4?

   A. 3 + 4 + 4 + 4
   B. 4 + 4 + 4 + 4
   C. 3 + 3
   D. 3 + 3 + 3 + 3

   3.OA.1

TIP of the DAY

If each group has the same amount of items in it, it's called an equal group. You can multiply the number of items in each group times the number of equal groups to find out how many total items you have.

WEEK 3 : DAY 2

1. Farmer Joe has 3 rows of corn. Each row has 6 plants on it. Which array represents how many corn plants Farmer Joe has?

   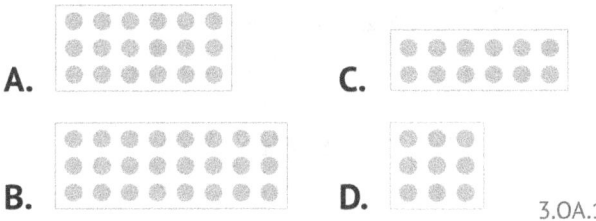

   A.
   B.
   C.
   D.

   3.OA.1

2. Which of the following expressions is *not equal* to the others?

   A. 6 × 4
   B. 12 × 2
   C. 8 × 3
   D. 10 × 3

   3.OA.1

3. Which expression could represent the total number of blue boxes?

   A. 5 + 2
   B. 5 × 2
   C. 10 × 2
   D. 10 + 2

   3.OA.1

4. Which picture represents 4 × 4?

   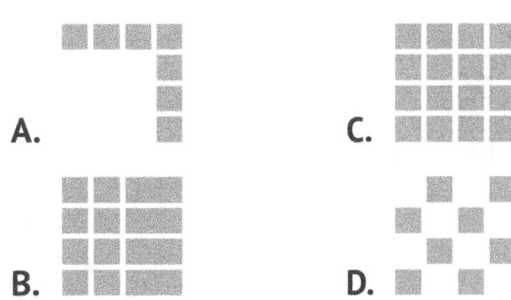

   A.
   B.
   C.
   D.

   3.OA.1

5. Which of the following statements is *true*?

   A. 5 + 5 + 5 = 5 × 2
   B. 5 + 5 + 5 = 5 × 3
   C. 5 + 5 + 5 + 5 = 5 + 4
   D. 5 + 5 + 3 = 5 × 3

   3.OA.1

TIP of the DAY

When solving multiplication problems, it helps to draw pictures or arrays to visualize the action in the problem. Practice turning an equation or situation into a picture or array.

WEEK 3 : DAY 3

1. What is the product of 4 × 50?

   A. 54
   B. 100
   C. 150
   D. 200

   3.NBT.3

2. Which equation shows the best way to find the product of 2 × 60?

   A. 2 × 6 = 12
   B. 2 × 60 = (2 × 6) × 10 = 12 × 10 = 120
   C. 2 + 60 = 62
   D. 2 × 6 × 10 = 18

   3.NBT.3

3. How much money would you have if there were 8 dimes in your pocket?

   A. 8 + 10 = 18 cents
   B. 8 + 8 = 16 cents
   C. (8 × 10) + 8 = 88 cents
   D. 8 × 10 = 80 cents

   3.NBT.3

4. Justine has 2 boxes with 19 shells in each box. Which equation shows **about** how many shells Justine has altogether, rounded to the nearest 10?

   A. 2 + 19 = 21 shells
   B. 2 + 20 = 22 shells
   C. 2 × 20 = 40 shells
   D. 2 × 19 = 38 shells

   3.NBT.1 / 3.OA.1

5. Below is one box of pencil holders that Mrs. Diaz bought at the store yesterday. If she bought 20 boxes, how many pencil holders did Mrs. Diaz buy altogether?

   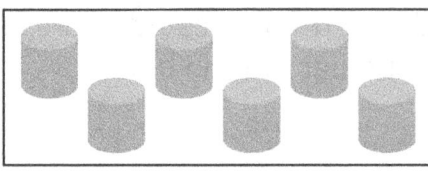

   A. 26 pencil holders
   B. 120 pencil holders
   C. 20 pencil holders
   D. 126 pencil holders

   3.NBT.3

TIP of the DAY

When multiplying by a multiple of 10, remember that you are multiplying by groups of ten. Therefore, just multiply by the digit in the tens place, then add a "0" on the end.
For example: 2 x 30 = 2 x 3 "tens" = 6 "tens" = 60!

WEEK 3 : DAY 4

1. Which expression best represents the picture below?

   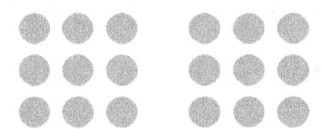

   A. 3 + 3
   B. 9 × 3
   C. 3 × 6
   D. 6 + 6

   3.OA.1

2. Mrs. Smith has 7 students and she gave each of them 8 pencils. Which expression represents how to find the number of pencils she gave out altogether?

   A. 7 + 8
   B. 7 + 7 + 7 + 7 + 7
   C. 8 + 8 + 8 + 8 + 8 + 8
   D. 8 + 8 + 8 + 8 + 8 + 8 + 8

   3.OA.1

3. Horatio has 7 dimes in his pocket. Does he have enough money to buy a piece of gum for 50 cents?

   A. Yes, he has 70 cents.
   B. Yes, he has 77 cents.
   C. No, he only has 17 cents.
   D. No, he only has 7 cents.

   3.NBT.3

4. What is the product of 8 and 70?

   A. 56
   B. 560
   C. 78
   D. 780

   3.NBT.3

5. Using the picture below, which number would complete the equation?

   $3 \times \square = 27$

   A. 27
   B. 3
   C. 9
   D. 12

   3.OA.1

TIP of the DAY

Multiplication often is identified by keywords like product, times, each, double, and every. Look out for these words when solving word problems!

WEEK 3 : DAY 5

ASSESSMENT

1. A gardener has 18 plants. Which picture could represent how his plants are arranged?

   3.OA.1

2. Which situation is best represented by the expression 3 × 7?

   A. 3 friends sit on a bench and 7 more friends come
   B. 3 friends share 7 crayons between them
   C. 3 friends have 7 boxes of crayons with 3 crayons in each box
   D. 3 friends each brought 7 crayons to share

   3.OA.1

3. Kelly has 586 red glass beads. She gives 245 away to her friends. **About** how many beads does she have left, rounded to the nearest 10?

   A. 341 beads   C. 340 beads
   B. 400 beads   D. 840 beads

   3.NBT.1 / 3.NBT.2

4. Danny has 5 stacks of baseball cards. Each stack has 30 cards in it. How many cards does Danny have altogether?

   A. 15 cards
   B. 35 cards
   C. 150 cards
   D. 80 cards

   3.OA.1 / 3.NBT.3

5. Which expression best represents the action on the number line below?

   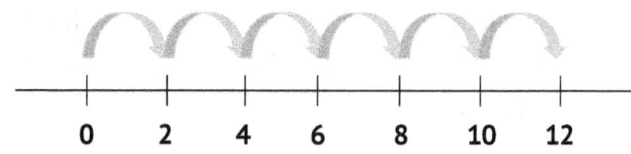

   A. 2 + 2 + 2
   B. 2 × 6
   C. 10 + 2
   D. 0 + 12

   3.OA.1

6. Which expression represents 6 boxes with 8 cupcakes in each box?

   A. 6 x 6
   B. 8 x 8
   C. 6 + 6 + 6 + 6 + 6 + 6
   D. 6 x 8

   3.OA.1

DAY 6 Challenge question

Kelsey is making gift bags that each have 3 lollipops and 5 pieces of gum. If she makes 9 bags, how many total pieces of candy did she put in the bags?

3.OA.1

This week you will make the connection between multiplication and division. As inverse operations, you will see that multiplication and division are related in many ways, as they both represent equal groups.
You can find detailed video explanations of each problem in the book by visiting: ArgoPrep.com

WEEK 4 : DAY 1

1. Which expression could represent the picture below?

   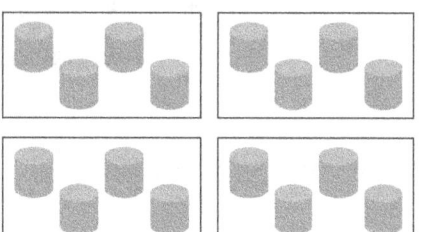

   A. 8 ÷ 2
   B. 8 ÷ 4
   C. 4 ÷ 16
   D. 16 ÷ 4

   3.OA.2

2. 36 students are in Mr. Kaine's class. If they are split into 6 equal groups, which equation represents how many students are in each group?

   A. 36 ÷ 6 = 6
   B. 6 + 6 = 12
   C. 36 × 6 = 216
   D. 36 - 6 = 30

   3.OA.2

3. Sheila has 20 balls total. She wants to divide them equally into 4 baskets. How many balls are in each basket?

   A. 4 balls
   B. 24 balls
   C. 5 balls
   D. 16 balls

   3.OA.2

4. Which of the following equations helps you to solve 56 ÷ 8?

   A. 8 × 8 = 64
   B. 8 × 7 = 56
   C. 56 - 8 = 48
   D. 56 + 8 = 64

   3.OA.2

5. Sheila has only dimes in her pocket. If she has 90 cents in her pocket, how many dimes does she have?

   A. 90 dimes
   B. 99 dimes
   C. 10 dimes
   D. 9 dimes

   3.OA.2 / 3.NBT.3

Multiplication and division are inverse operations. If you know that 4 × 6 = 24, then you can figure out that 24 ÷ 6 = 4 or that 24 ÷ 4 = 6.

WEEK 4 : DAY 2

1. There are 27 marbles being shared equally among 3 children. How many marbles will each child get?

   A. 3 × 27 = 81
   B. 3 + 27 = 30
   C. 27 ÷ 3 = 9
   D. 3 ÷ 9 = 27

   3.OA.2

2. What is the quotient of 35 ÷ 5?

   A. 5
   B. 7
   C. 30
   D. 40

   3.OA.2

3. There are 30 marbles in the collection. There are 5 different colors of marbles, and an equal amount of each color. How many marbles are there in each color?

   A. 35 marbles
   B. 25 marbles
   C. 6 marbles
   D. 5 marbles

   3.OA.2

4. Which situation could be represented by the picture below?

   A. 5 friends each bring 20 books to share.
   B. 5 friends each bring 5 books to share.
   C. 20 books are shared equally among 4 friends.
   D. 20 books are shared equally among 5 friends.

   3.OA.2

5. Wilson bought 21 tennis balls altogether. The tennis balls came in packs of 3. How many packs of tennis balls did Wilson buy?

   A. 24 packs
   B. 18 packs
   C. 7 packs
   D. 8 packs

   3.OA.2

6. What is the quotient of 42 ÷ 6?

   A. 6   C. 8
   B. 7   D. 9

   3.OA.2

Draw pictures and arrays if you need help with division. Representing a situation with visuals makes division easier!

WEEK 4 : DAY 3

1. Which expression could be represented by the picture below?

   A. 4 × 24
   B. 4 ÷ 24
   C. 6 ÷ 24
   D. 24 ÷ 4

   3.OA.2

2. Hank made 20 cookies in his first batch and 20 cookies in his second batch. If he gives an equal amount of cookies to 4 friends, how many will each friend get?

   A. 44   C. 10
   B. 40   D. 14

   3.OA.2

3. Which of the following expressions helps you to solve 64 ÷ 8?

   A. 8 × 8 = 64
   B. 8 + 8 = 16
   C. 64 × 8 = 512
   D. 64 + 8 = 72

   3.OA.2

4. If Sam divides 48 pens equally among 8 cups, how many pens will be in each cup?

   A. 5
   B. 6
   C. 7
   D. 8

   3.OA.2

5. Which of the following statements is *false*?

   A. 15 ÷ 1 = 15
   B. 12 ÷ 3 = 4
   C. 15 ÷ 5 = 10
   D. 12 ÷ 6 = 2

   3.OA.2

6. What is the quotient of 70 ÷ 7?

   A. 7
   B. 8
   C. 9
   D. 10

   3.OA.2 / 3.NBT.3

TIP of the DAY

When finding a quotient, think about the multiplication facts that could help you. For example, if you know 4 × 7 = 28, then you can figure out the quotient of 28 ÷ 7.

WEEK 4 : DAY 4

1. Rosco has 28 bones in his dog house. He wants to put his bones into 4 equal stacks. How many bones will be in each stack?

   A. 32 bones
   B. 24 bones
   C. 8 bones
   D. 7 bones

   3.OA.2

2. Which of the following statements is true?

   A. 4 ÷ 8 = 32
   B. 32 ÷ 4 = 8
   C. 8 ÷ 4 = 32
   D. 32 ÷ 4 = 36

   3.OA.2

3. The Donut Shop sells donuts in boxes of 12. If each person eats 2 donuts, how many people can eat donuts from two boxes?

   A. 24 people
   B. 12 people
   C. 8 people
   D. 6 people

   3.OA.2

4. What is the quotient of 72 ÷ 9?

   A. 81
   B. 63
   C. 7
   D. 8

   3.OA.2

5. Which situation best describes the picture represented below?

   A. 15 beads are shared equally with 5 friends.
   B. 15 beads are shared equally with 3 friends.
   C. 5 beads are shared equally with 3 friends.
   D. 3 beads are shared equally with 5 friends.

   3.OA.2

6. Which equation can be solved by knowing that 6 × 9 = 54?

   A. 9 ÷ 54 =
   B. 6 ÷ 54 =
   C. 54 × 6 =
   D. 54 ÷ 9 =

   3.OA.2 / 3.NBT.3

TIP of the DAY

In division, you always have to make sure that items are shared equally. For example, if sharing 6 items between 2 groups, each group must be given an equal amount, or 3 items each.

WEEK 4 : DAY 5

ASSESSMENT

1. Nine students will equally share 81 pencils. How many pencils will each student get?

   A. 6 pencils
   B. 7 pencils
   C. 8 pencils
   D. 9 pencils

   3.OA.2

2. Which equation could be represented by the picture below?

   A. 24 ÷ 6 = 4
   B. 24 ÷ 6 = 6
   C. 4 ÷ 24 = 6
   D. 6 ÷ 24 = 4

   3.OA.2

3. Which situation could be represented by 7 × 6 = 42?

   A. 7 friends each have 42 beads
   B. 6 friends each have 42 beads
   C. 7 friends have 6 beads altogether
   D. 7 friends each have 6 beads

   3.OA.1

4. There are 345 girls and 487 boys at summer camp. *About* how many kids are at summer camp altogether, rounded to the nearest 10?

   A. 832
   B. 830
   C. 840
   D. 820

   3.NBT.1 / 3.NBT.2

5. What is the quotient of 63 ÷ 9?

   A. 5
   B. 6
   C. 7
   D. 8

   3.OA.2

6. Jamal and his 4 friends will share 20 pieces of gum equally. How many pieces of gum will each person get?

   A. 3
   B. 4
   C. 5
   D. 6

   3.OA.2

DAY 6
Challenge question

There are 6 bags of candy with 4 pieces of candy in each. If Hannah wants to give each friend 2 pieces of candy, how many friends can she give candy to?

3.OA.2

36

WEEK 5

Week 5 will give you even more opportunities to practice your multiplication and division facts. By using Fact Families, you will be able to re-write multiplication sentences as division sentences, and vice versa. Real-world problems will be a big focus.

You can find detailed video explanations of each problem in the book by visiting: ArgoPrep.com

WEEK 5 : DAY 1

1. Janie is having a birthday party. She buys 7 packs of hot dogs with 8 hot dogs in each pack. How many hot dogs is Janie planning to make?

   A. 15 hot dogs
   B. 49 hot dogs
   C. 56 hot dogs
   D. 64 hot dogs

   3.OA.3

2. There are 5 baskets below with cookies in them. How many cookies are there in all?

   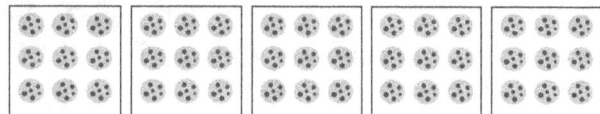

   A. 5 × 5 = 25 cookies
   B. 5 × 9 = 45 cookies
   C. 5 ÷ 45 = 9 cookies
   D. 9 ÷ 45 = 5 cookies

   3.OA.3

3. Jeff sees 9 horses in the stable. How many legs does Jeff see?

   A. 9 + 9 + 9 = 27 legs
   B. 9 × 2 = 18 legs
   C. 4 × 2 = 8 legs
   D. 9 × 4 = 36 legs

   3.OA.3

4. Which situation could be represented by the equation 36 ÷ 6 = 6?

   A. 36 baskets with 6 biscuits in each basket
   B. 6 baskets with 36 biscuits in each basket
   C. 36 biscuits shared equally among 6 baskets
   D. 6 biscuits shared equally among 36 baskets

   3.OA.3

5. Which equation best represents the array below?

   A. 18 ÷ 6 = 3
   B. 18 ÷ 3 = 3
   C. 6 ÷ 18 = 3
   D. 3 ÷ 18 = 6

   3.OA.3

6. Hallie made 11 gift bags with candy. Each gift bag looked like this:

   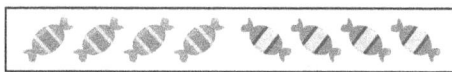

   How many pieces of candy did Hallie put in the gift bags altogether?

   A. 8 pieces
   B. 19 pieces
   C. 11 pieces
   D. 88 pieces

   3.OA.3

TIP of the DAY

When reading a word problem, make sure to determine which math operation the action in the problem represents: multiplication, division, addition, or subtraction!

WEEK 5 : DAY 2

1. Harry buys 24 popsicles. If he gives 2 popsicles to each of his students, how many students can he give popsicles to?

   A. 26 students
   B. 12 students
   C. 11 students
   D. 10 students

   3.OA.4

2. Sarah Jane swims 12 laps every day. If she has swam 84 laps so far this month, how many days has she swam?

   A. 7 days
   B. 96 days
   C. 8 days
   D. 72 days

   3.OA.4

3. Judy's garden has 6 rows of rose bushes. Each row has 9 rose bushes in it. How many rose bushes does Judy have?

   A. 45 rose bushes
   B. 54 rose bushes
   C. 55 rose bushes
   D. 63 rose bushes

   3.OA.4

4. Which two numbers are missing from the equation based on the array below?

   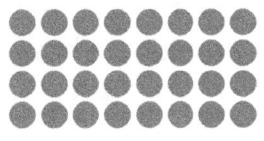

   $\Box \div 4 = \Box$

   A. 4 and 8
   B. 32 and 4
   C. 32 and 8
   D. 8 and 8

   3.OA.4

5. Mr. James made two batches of cookies. Each batch had 10 cookies. If he gives away all the cookies equally to 4 friends, how many cookies will each friend receive?

   A. 20 cookies
   B. 24 cookies
   C. 6 cookies
   D. 5 cookies

   3.OA.4

6. Tennis balls come in packages of 3 balls in each. If Joan sold 30 tennis balls altogether, how many packages did she sell?

   A. 11 packages
   B. 10 packages
   C. 33 packages
   D. 3 packages

   3.OA.4

TIP of the DAY

Drawing arrays is similar to drawing equal groups. If you put the same number of items in each row, they create equal groups of items, and are easy to count!

WEEK 5 : DAY 3

1. The picture below shows Kassie's box of envelopes. If she **doubled** the amount of envelopes she has in the box, how many envelopes would she have?

   A. 16 envelopes
   B. 18 envelopes
   C. 32 envelopes
   D. 34 envelopes

   3.OA.3

2. Julian bought 72 marbles. If he wants to divide them equally between 8 bags, which equation represents how many marbles will be in each bag?

   A. 72 + 8 = 80
   B. 8 ÷ 72 = 9
   C. 9 ÷ 72 = 8
   D. 72 ÷ 8 = 9

   3.OA.4

3. Which expression best represents the picture below?

   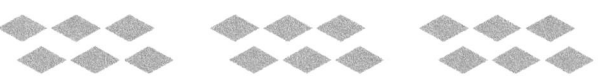

   A. 18 ÷ 3 = 6
   B. 3 × 18 = 6
   C. 6 ÷ 3 = 18
   D. 6 ÷ 18 = 3

   3.OA.3

4. Jerrell has 3 shelves to put his books on equally. If he has 27 books, how many books will go on each shelf?

   A. 6 books
   B. 7 books
   C. 8 books
   D. 9 books

   3.OA.4

5. Which situation best represents the equation 64 ÷ 8?

   A. 8 baskets with 64 crayons in each basket
   B. 64 baskets with 8 crayons in each basket
   C. 64 crayons placed equally in 8 baskets
   D. 8 crayons placed equally in 64 baskets

   3.OA.3

6. There are 5 days in a work week. Mrs. Hansen walks the same amount of miles every day to work. If she walks 30 miles in one work week, how many miles does she walk each day?

   A. 5 miles
   B. 6 miles
   C. 35 miles
   D. 25 miles

   3.OA.4

TIP of the DAY

Division can often be solved by knowing your multiplication facts. 54 ÷ 9 is a lot easier if you know that 9 × 6 = 54.

WEEK 5 : DAY 4

1. Toy cars come in packs of 6. Owen bought 42 toy cars today. How many packs of toy cars did Owen buy?

   A. 4 packs
   B. 5 packs
   C. 6 packs
   D. 7 packs

   3.OA.4

2. Mr. Ellis walked 7 laps this morning and it took him 49 minutes total. If each lap took an equal amount of time to walk, how many minutes did each lap take?

   A. 6 minutes
   B. 7 minutes
   C. 8 minutes
   D. 9 minutes

   3.OA.4

3. Which equation best represents the picture below?

   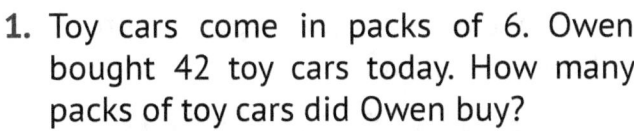

   A. 8 ÷ 24 = 3
   B. 3 ÷ 24 = 8
   C. 24 ÷ 3 = 3
   D. 24 ÷ 3 = 8

   3.OA.3

4. The bike shop just got 18 new tires. If each bike needs two tires, how many bikes can they put new tires on?

   A. 20 bikes
   B. 16 bikes
   C. 9 bikes
   D. 8 bikes

   3.OA.4

5. Kaitlin has two packs of markers, each with 15 markers in it. If she gives away the markers equally to 6 friends, how many markers will each friend get?

   A. 30 markers
   B. 36 markers
   C. 5 markers
   D. 6 markers

   3.OA.4

6. Which situation is best represented by 5 × 9 = 45?

   A. 45 students each bring 9 pencils
   B. 5 students each bring 9 pencils
   C. 5 students each bring 45 pencils
   D. 9 students each bring 45 pencils

   3.OA.3

TIP of the DAY

The Commutative Property of Multiplication says that the order in which you multiply two numbers doesn't matter. For example, 6 × 8 = 48 is the same as 8 × 6 = 48.

WEEK 5 : DAY 5

ASSESSMENT

1. Golf Carts have 4 wheels each. If Raul sees 28 wheels in the Golf Cart shop, how many Golf Carts are there?

   A. 5 Golf Carts
   B. 6 Golf Carts
   C. 7 Golf Carts
   D. 8 Golf Carts

   3.OA.4

2. Carolyn bought pencils in packs of 10. She first bought 3 packs, then went back and bought 4 more. How many pencils did Carolyn buy in all?

   A. 17 pencils
   B. 70 pencils
   C. 77 pencils
   D. 7 pencils

   3.OA.1 / 3.NBT.3

3. A box of fruit has 349 apples and 293 pears in it. **About** how much fruit is in the box, rounded to the nearest 10?

   A. 642
   B. 640
   C. 650
   D. 600

   3.NBT.1 / 3.NBT.3

4. Which two equations could represent the array below?

   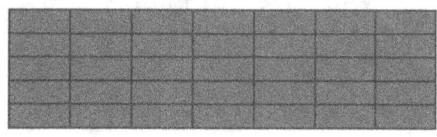

   A. 5 × 7 = 35 and 5 ÷ 7 = 35
   B. 5 × 7 = 35 and 7 ÷ 5 = 35
   C. 7 × 5 = 35 and 35 ÷ 5 = 7
   D. 7 × 5 = 35 and 35 ÷ 7 = 7

   3.OA.3 / 3.OA.4

5. The baker has 3 shelves to put his pastries on equally. He just made two dozen pastries. How many pastries will go on each shelf?

   A. 24 pastries
   B. 27 pastries
   C. 7 pastries
   D. 8 pastries

   3.OA.4

6. What is the product of 8 and 7?

   A. 15
   B. 63
   C. 64
   D. 56

   3.OA.1

DAY 6
Challenge question

Ralph bought 3 dozen donuts for the party. If he arranges them on 6 plates, how many donuts will be on each plate?

3.OA.3 / 4

WEEK 6

VIDEO EXPLANATIONS — ARGOPREP.COM

Properties of multiplication and division will be covered in Week 6. Learning about the Commutative, Associative, and Distributive Properties will help you in solving challenging multiplication and division problems down the road.

You can find detailed video explanations of each problem in the book by visiting: ArgoPrep.com

WEEK 6 : DAY 1

1. Which equation is represented by the picture below?

   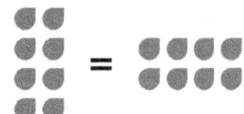

   A. 4 + 4 = 2 + 2 + 2
   B. 4 × 2 = 2 × 4
   C. 4 × 4 = 2 × 2
   D. 4 + 4 = 2 + 2

   3.OA.5

2. Which of the following statements is *false*?

   A. 2 × 5 = 5 × 2
   B. 6 + 6 = 2 × 6
   C. 3 × 4 = 4 × 3
   D. 3 + 3 = 3 × 4

   3.OA.5

3. Which situation could be represented by 2 × 5 = 5 × 2?

   A. 2 rows of 5 plants or 5 rows of 2 plants
   B. 2 rows with 5 plants and 5 trees in each
   C. 5 rows with 2 plants and 2 trees in each
   D. 5 rows with 2 plants and 2 rows with 2 plants

   3.OA.5

4. Which of the following equations **would not** represent the picture below?

   A. 3 × 8 = 24
   B. 8 × 3 = 24
   C. 24 ÷ 3 = 8
   D. 3 ÷ 24 = 8

   3.OA.5

5. Sara thinks 5 baskets with 4 balls each is equal to 4 baskets with 5 balls each. Is she correct?

   A. Yes, because 5 × 5 is equal to 4 × 4.
   B. Yes, because 5 × 4 is equal to 4 × 5.
   C. No, because 5 × 5 is not equal to 4 × 4.
   D. No, because 5 × 4 is not equal to 4 × 5.

   3.OA.5

6. Which number is missing from the equation below?

   ☐ × 2 = 2 × 9

   A. 18
   B. 11
   C. 2
   D. 9

   3.OA.5

TIP of the DAY

The Commutative Property of Multiplication says that even if you change the order of two numbers being multiplied, you will always end up with the same product. So, 3 × 2 = 6 and 2 × 3 = 6.

WEEK 6 : DAY 2

1. Which of the equations is *false*?

   A. 2 × 3 × 5 = 2 × 5 × 3
   B. 2 × 3 × 5 = 5 × 3 × 2
   C. 2 × 3 × 5 = 3 × 5 × 2
   D. 2 × 3 × 5 = 5 × 3 × 3

   3.OA.5

2. Which number is missing from the equation below?

   ☐ × 4 × 5 = 5 × 6 × 4

   A. 4
   B. 5
   C. 6
   D. 7

   3.OA.5

3. If 3 × 4 × 6 = 72, what is the product of 6 × 4 × 3?

   A. 13
   B. 24
   C. 12
   D. 72

   3.OA.5

4. Kelley has 6 crayons and 2 markers in each box. If she has 5 boxes, how many crayons and markers does she have altogether?

   A. 12
   B. 10
   C. 40
   D. 30

   3.OA.5

5. What is the product of 2 × 3 × 8?

   A. 92
   B. 48
   C. 24
   D. 12

   3.OA.5

6. Which equation below could be true using the numbers 2, 3, and 7?

   A. 2 × 3 × 7 = 7 × 3 × 2
   B. 2 × 3 × 7 = 2 + 3 + 7
   C. 2 × 3 × 7 = 2 × 3 + 7
   D. 2 × 3 × 7 = 2 + 3 × 7

   3.OA.5

TIP of the DAY

The Associative Property of Multiplication says that the product of a set of 3 or more numbers is the same, no matter how they are grouped.
For example 2 × (5 × 3) = 30 and (3 × 5) × 2 = 30.

WEEK 6 : DAY 3

1. Do the two pictures below show the same amount?

   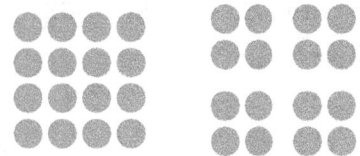

   A. No, because 4 × 4 is not equal to 2 × 2.
   B. No, because 4 × 4 is not equal to 4 × (2 × 2).
   C. Yes, because 4 × 4 is equal to 4 × (2 × 2).
   D. Yes, because 4 × 4 is equal to 2 × 2.

   3.OA.5

2. Using the distributive property, what is the product of 2 × (3 + 4)?

   A. 10 C. 12
   B. 6   D. 14

   3.OA.5

3. Which equation is represented by the picture below?

   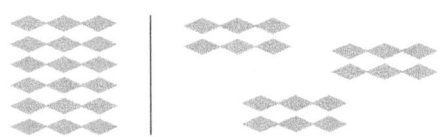

   A. 3 × 6 = 3 × 3   C. 3 × 6 = 6 × 2
   B. 3 × 6 = 6 × 3   D. 3 × 6 = 6 + 6

   3.OA.5

4. Which of the following expressions is equal to 2 × 5?

   A. 2 + 5
   B. 2 × (5 + 2)
   C. 2 × (2 + 3)
   D. 5 × (2 + 3)

   3.OA.5

5. What is the product of 4 × (2 + 7)?

   A. 36
   B. 28
   C. 14
   D. 15

   3.OA.5

6. Janell has 5 boxes. Each box has 3 red beads and 6 blue beads. Which equations represents how many beads Janell has altogether?

   A. 5 × 3 + 6 = 21 beads
   B. 5 × (3 + 6) = (5 × 3) + (5 × 6) = 45 beads
   C. 5 × 3 + 3 × 6 = 33 beads
   D. 3 × 6 + 5 = 23 beads

   3.OA.5

TIP of the DAY

The Distributive Property of Multiplication says that a multiplication expression can be divided into two smaller expressions. For example, 2 × 11 could be written as 2 × (5 + 6).

WEEK 6 : DAY 4

1. Which of the following equations *would not* represent the picture below?

   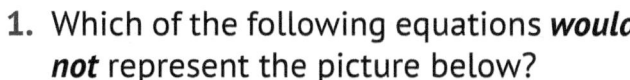

   A. 4 × 8 = 32
   B. 8 × 4 = 32
   C. 4 ÷ 32 = 8
   D. 32 ÷ 4 = 8

   3.OA.5

2. Kaylen can either buy 2 packs of markers for $5 each or 5 packs of pens for $2 each. Which is going to be more expensive?

   A. The markers will be more expensive, because they are $5.
   B. The markers will be more expensive, because 2 × $5 = $10.
   C. The pens will be more expensive, because 5 × $2 = $10.
   D. The markers and pens will be the same price because 5 × $2 = 2 × $5.

   3.OA.5

3. Farmer Dale wants to put 18 rose bushes in equal rows. Which equation *does not* represent one way he could arrange his rose bushes?

   A. 3 × 6 = 18   C. 6 × 3 = 18
   B. 6 ÷ 18 = 3   D. 18 ÷ 6 = 3

   3.OA.5

4. If you *double* the amount of apples in each of the boxes below, how many apples would you have?

   A. 5 × 2 = 5 + 5 = 10 apples
   B. 4 × 2 = 4 + 4 = 8 apples
   C. 5 × 4 = 5 + 5 + 5 + 5 = 20 apples
   D. 2 × (5 + 4) = (2 × 5) + (2 × 4) = = 18 apples

   3.OA.5

5. Which of the following statements is *true*?

   A. 5 × 3 × 6 = 3 × 5 × 6
   B. 2 × (3 + 7) = 7 × (2 + 3)
   C. 1 + 5 + 7 = 5 × 1 × 7
   D. 25 × 5 = 5 + (20 + 5)

   3.OA.5

Try using the Distributive Property of Multiplication to make challenging problems easier. You can break (15 × 3) into [(10 × 3) + (5 × 3)] which will be 30 + 15 = 45.

47

WEEK 6 : DAY 5

ASSESSMENT

1. Which number is missing from the equation below?

    $4 \times (5 \times 9) = (4 \times \boxed{}) \times 9$

    A. 4
    B. 5
    C. 9
    D. 20

    3.OA.5

2. Which of the following equations **does not** represent the picture below?

    A. 9 ÷ 18 = 2
    B. 18 ÷ 2 = 9
    C. 2 × 9 = 18
    D. 9 × 2 = 18

    3.OA.5

3. Jessamyn has 4 boxes of crayons. If there are 39 in each box, **about** how many crayons does she have total?

    A. 43 crayons
    B. 40 crayons
    C. 160 crayons
    D. 150 crayons

    3.NBT.1 / 3.NBT.3

4. What is the product of 4 × (3 + 6)?

    A. 12
    B. 36
    C. 24
    D. 13

    3.OA.5

5. Sammy has boxes that store 5 marbles each. If he has 45 marbles total, how many boxes does Sammy need to store all his marbles?

    A. 50 boxes
    B. 40 boxes
    C. 8 boxes
    D. 9 boxes

    3.OA.3 / 3.OA.4

6. Which equation is represented by the picture below?

    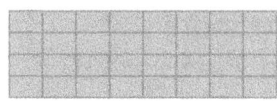 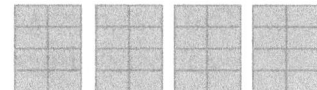

    A. 4 × 8 = 4 × 4
    B. 4 × 8 = 8 × 4
    C. 4 × 8 = (4 × 2) + 4
    D. 4 × 8 = 8 × 2

    3.OA.5

DAY 6 Challenge question

There is a box with 9 basketballs, 7 baseballs, and 5 tennis balls. If you were to **double** the amount of each type of ball, how many total balls would you have? Round that number to the nearest 10.

3.OA.5

48

WEEK 7

Week 7 includes many real-world problems using multiplication and division. This week will be a great way to see if you are truly making the connection between multiplication and division, and using that connection to help you solve equations with unknown factors.

You can find detailed video explanations of each problem in the book by visiting: ArgoPrep.com

WEEK 7 : DAY 1

1. Joni earned $28 babysitting last night. If she charges $7 for each hour she babysits, how many hours did she babysit?

   A. 3 hours
   B. 4 hours
   C. 5 hours
   D. 6 hours

   3.OA.6

2. What is the quotient of 56 ÷ 8?

   A. 5
   B. 6
   C. 7
   D. 8

   3.OA.6

3. Mr. Johnson puts 6 cupcakes on each plate for the party. If there are 54 cupcakes total, how many plates will he need for all the cupcakes?

   A. 5 plates
   B. 6 plates
   C. 8 plates
   D. 9 plates

   3.OA.6

4. Which situation could be represented by the following picture?

   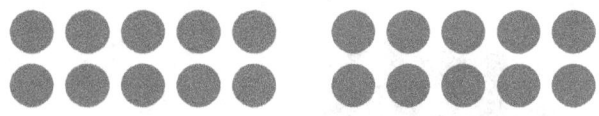

   A. 5 shelves each have 2 books on them
   B. 2 shelves each have 5 books on them
   C. 10 shelves each have 5 books on them
   D. 2 shelves each have 10 books on them

   3.OA.6

5. Which of the following equations is *true*?

   A. 5 × 3 = 5 + 5 + 5 + 5
   B. 4 × 3 = 3 + 3 + 3
   C. 2 + 2 + 2 + 2 + 2 = 2 × 5
   D. 7 + 7 + 7 + 7 = 4 + 7

   3.OA.6

6. What is the product of 8 and 7?

   A. 56
   B. 54
   C. 63
   D. 45

   3.OA.6

Fact Families are related multiplication and division facts, like 4 × 5 = 20 and 20 ÷ 4 = 5. Use fact families to help you solve more challenging problems.

WEEK 7 : DAY 2

1. Which of the following equations is *false*?

   A. 5 × 7 = 35
   B. 7 × 9 = 63
   C. 54 ÷ 6 = 9
   D. 36 ÷ 6 = 4

   3.OA.7

2. Catherine has 6 boxes of clothes. She has 3 pairs of pants and 4 shirts in each box. How many pieces of clothing does she have altogether?

   A. 42
   B. 40
   C. 36
   D. 24

   3.OA.7

3. The library is open for 35 hours each week. The library is open for the same amount of hours each day. If the library is open for 5 days a week, how many hours is the library open each day?

   A. 4 hours
   B. 5 hours
   C. 6 hours
   D. 7 hours

   3.OA.7

4. Cal volunteers 12 hours a week. Each time he volunteers for 3 hours. How many times a week does Cal volunteer?

   A. 3 times
   B. 4 times
   C. 5 times
   D. 6 times

   3.OA.7

5. Julius makes boxes of fruit. One box is shown below. If Julius makes 9 boxes, how many pieces of fruit will he need in all?

   A. 56   C. 70
   B. 63   D. 54

   3.OA.7

6. Neil needs to buy gifts for each of his 8 friends. He spends 5 dollars on a gift and 1 dollar on a card for each of them. How much money will he spend altogether?

   A. 40 dollars   C. 48 dollars
   B. 45 dollars   D. 42 dollars

   3.OA.7

TIP of the DAY

If you are stumped by a multiplication fact, try breaking it into two smaller problems. For example, 4 × 7 is the same as 4 × (5 + 2). Then add the products of 4 × 5 and 4 × 2 together.

WEEK 7 : DAY 3

1. What is the quotient of 54 ÷ 9?

    A. 4
    B. 5
    C. 6
    D. 7

    3.OA.6

2. Henry bought 32 pieces of candy at the shop. He bought 8 of each type of candy. How many types of candy did he buy?

    A. 3
    B. 4
    C. 5
    D. 6

    3.OA.6

3. Which equation **would not** represent the array below?

    A. 4 × 7 = 28
    B. 7 × 4 = 28
    C. 28 ÷ 7 = 4
    D. 4 ÷ 28 = 7

    3.OA.7

4. Mr. Bretson always passes out 2 pieces of candy to each of his students. If he has 14 pieces of candy left, how many students can he pass out candy to?

    A. 8 students
    B. 7 students
    C. 6 students
    D. 5 students

    3.OA.6

5. Kamil walks 4 miles to school every day. If he has been to school 9 days so far this month, how many miles has he walked to school?

    A. 27 miles
    B. 45 miles
    C. 36 miles
    D. 40 miles

    3.OA.7

6. If you were to **double** the amount of stars below, how many stars would you have in all?

    A. 12 C. 36
    B. 24 D. 48

    3.OA.7

TIP of the DAY

In division, using fact families can help you figure out unknown numbers in an equation. If asked to solve 42 ÷ 6, use your fact families to remember that 6 × 7 = 42, so 42 ÷ 6 = 7.

WEEK 7 : DAY 4

1. The 3rd Grade has 6 classes. Each class has 8 computers in their classroom. How many computers does the 3rd Grade have?

    A. 36 computers
    B. 42 computers
    C. 48 computers
    D. 54 computers

    3.OA.6

2. Yemi has 36 photos. He can put 3 photos on each page in his album. How many pages does he need to fit all of his photos?

    A. 9 pages
    B. 10 pages
    C. 11 pages
    D. 12 pages

    3.OA.6

3. What is the product of 4 and 11?

    A. 4
    B. 40
    C. 44
    D. 14

    3.OA.7

4. Which expression has a quotient of 7?

    A. 64 ÷ 8
    B. 49 ÷ 7
    C. 54 ÷ 9
    D. 72 ÷ 8

    3.OA.6

5. Samantha has 36 beads that she wants to place equally on 6 necklaces. How many beads will be on each necklace?

    A. 4 beads
    B. 5 beads
    C. 6 beads
    D. 7 beads

    3.OA.6

6. Which equation represents the picture below?

    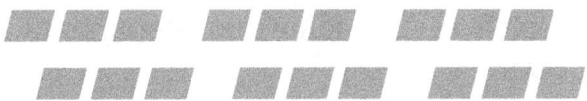

    A. 18 ÷ 3 = 6
    B. 18 ÷ 3 = 3
    C. 6 ÷ 18 = 3
    D. 3 ÷ 18 = 6

    3.OA.6 / 3.OA.7

TIP of the DAY

Drawing arrays and pictures can help you to solve division or equal sharing problems. Decide how many equal groups you need, and divide the total amount evenly among them.

WEEK 7 : DAY 5

ASSESSMENT

1. Beth made $64 cutting hair yesterday. She charged $8 for each haircut. How many haircuts did she give?

   A. 6 haircuts
   B. 7 haircuts
   C. 8 haircuts
   D. 9 haircuts

   3.OA.6 / 3.OA.7

2. Mr. Alvarez made 3 batches of cookies. Each batch had 12 cookies in it. If he stores the cookies equally in 6 bags, how many cookies will be in each bag?

   A. 36 cookies
   B. 24 cookies
   C. 8 cookies
   D. 6 cookies

   3.OA.6 / 3.OA.7

3. Which of the following statements is *true*?

   A. 4 × 5 = 5 + 5 + 5 + 5 + 5
   B. 2 + 2 + 2 + 2 = 4 × 2
   C. 2 × 3 = 3 + 3 + 3
   D. 4 × 7 = 4 + 7 + 7 + 7 + 7

   3.OA.5

4. Mr. Falken packs cups into boxes. One of the boxes is shown below. If he packs 11 boxes, how many cups will he have packed?

   A. 90 cups   C. 81 cups
   B. 99 cups   D. 91 cups

   3.OA.6 / 3.OA.7

5. Each month swimmers go to swim practice 10 times. They swim for 11 months a year. How many swim practices do they go to each year?

   A. 100 practices   C. 111 practices
   B. 101 practices   D. 110 practices

   3.OA.6 / 3.NBT.3

6. Kevin has 56 raffle tickets to give out. He wants to pass them out equally to the 8 neighbors on his street. How many tickets can he give each neighbor?

   A. 6 tickets   C. 8 tickets
   B. 7 tickets   D. 9 tickets

   3.OA.6 / 3.OA.7

DAY 6 Challenge question

Thomas goes to basketball practice 6 times a month and piano practice 6 times a month. If he goes for 12 months, how many times will he have gone to basketball and piano practice altogether?

3.OA.6

54

WEEK 8

VIDEO EXPLANATIONS

ARGOPREP.COM

This week will provide opportunities to solve multi-step word problems using all four operations. Week 8 will also cover arithmetic patterns including all four operations, allowing you to recognize and continue patterns in different situations.

You can find detailed video explanations of each problem in the book by visiting: ArgoPrep.com

WEEK 8 : DAY 1

1. Jason needs $20 to get a new stereo. He has $5 already. If he gets $5 allowance each week, how many more weeks will he need to save his allowance to afford the stereo?

   A. 3 weeks
   B. 4 weeks
   C. 5 weeks
   D. 6 weeks

   3.OA.8

2. Hvar has 98 bunches of flowers to sell. He sold 45 bunches this morning, and 23 this afternoon. How many flowers does he have left to sell?

   A. 68 bunches
   B. 53 bunches
   C. 75 bunches
   D. 30 bunches

   3.OA.8

3. There are 3 dozen donuts in the kitchen this morning. This afternoon there were only 14 left. How many donuts were eaten this morning?

   A. 36 donuts
   B. 22 donuts
   C. 23 donuts
   D. 20 donuts

   3.OA.8

4. There are 52 weeks in a year. Four times a year the Smiths go on vacation for 2 weeks. How many weeks of the year are they *not* on vacation?

   A. 8 weeks
   B. 2 weeks
   C. 44 weeks
   D. 42 weeks

   3.OA.8

5. Ashley has 123 beads. Sheldon has twice as many beads as Ashley. How many beads do they have altogether?

   A. 246 beads
   B. 245 beads
   C. 368 beads
   D. 369 beads

   3.OA.8

6. James bought 6 packs of hot dogs with 8 hot dogs in each pack. If 25 hot dogs were eaten, how many hot dogs were not eaten?

   A. 23 hot dogs
   B. 48 hot dogs
   C. 17 hot dogs
   D. 25 hot dogs

   3.OA.8

TIP of the DAY

When solving multi-step word problems, re-read the problem to make sure you know which step is the right place to start.

WEEK 8 : DAY 2

1. Which statement best describes the pattern below?

    3, 6, 9, 12, 15, 18, 21…

    A. Multiples of 2, or add 2
    B. Multiples of 3, or add 3
    C. Multiples of 4, or add 4
    D. Multiples of 6, or add 6

    3.OA.9

2. Which pattern can be described by "multiples of 4"?

    A. 4, 8, 12, 15, 19
    B. 4, 8, 10, 14, 18
    C. 4, 8, 12, 16, 22
    D. 4, 8, 12, 16, 20

    3.OA.9

3. Janell does 12 pushups on Monday, 24 on Tuesday, and 36 on Wednesday. If this pattern continues, how many pushups will Janell do on Friday?

    A. 48 pushups
    B. 60 pushups
    C. 72 pushups
    D. 12 pushups

    3.OA.9

4. The table below shows how many movie tickets were sold this week.

Day of the week	Tickets Sold
Monday	4
Tuesday	8
Wednesday	16
Thursday	32

    What pattern best describes the ticket sales?

    A. Each day 4 more tickets are sold than the day before.
    B. Each day 8 more tickets are sold than the day before.
    C. Each day twice as many tickets are sold as the day before.
    D. Each day three times as many tickets are sold as the day before.

    3.OA.9

5. Which of these patterns *does not* follow the rule "add 6"?

    A. 3, 9, 15, 22
    B. 2, 8, 14, 20
    C. 5, 11, 17, 23
    D. 6, 12, 18, 24

    3.OA.9

TIP of the DAY

When looking for patterns, think about how the numbers change. If they increase, you might be adding or multiplying each time. If they decrease, you might be subtracting or dividing each time.

WEEK 8 : DAY 3

1. The chart below shows how many cupcakes Jena makes.

May	June	July	August
15	30	45	60

   If the pattern continues, how many cupcakes will Jena make in October?

   A. 75 cupcakes C. 30 cupcakes
   B. 90 cupcakes D. 95 cupcakes

   3.OA.8 / 3.OA.9

2. Harris has two boxes, each with 123 tomatoes. If he sells 112 tomatoes at the market, how many tomatoes does he have left?

   A. 11 tomatoes   C. 134 tomatoes
   B. 246 tomatoes D. 112 tomatoes

   3.OA.8

3. Mr. Bates collects 6 rocks on Monday, 12 rocks on Tuesday, and 24 rocks on Wednesday. If the pattern continues, and he collects rocks on Thursday and Friday, how many rocks will he have collected in all?

   A. 42 rocks   C. 48 rocks
   B. 36 rocks   D. 186 rocks

   3.OA.9

4. Which statement best describes the pattern below?

   12, 20, 28, 36, 44

   A. Add 12 each time
   B. Add 10 each time
   C. Add 8 each time
   D. Add 6 each time

   3.OA.9

5. Jayla found the product of 4 and 5, and Kallie found the product of 6 and 7. What is the sum of both of their products?

   A. 62
   B. 68
   C. 48
   D. 42

   3.OA.7 / 3.OA.8

6. Every year, Hillary grows 2 inches. If she is 36 inches now, how many inches will she be in 3 years?

   A. 40 inches
   B. 42 inches
   C. 44 inches
   D. 46 inches

   3.OA.8 / 3.OA.9

TIP of the DAY

Circle keywords or actions in word problems. Re-read your word problem to see if there are keywords to help you solve it.

WEEK 8 : DAY 4

1. The Bread Shop wants to sell 165 loaves before the end of the day. They sold 83 this morning and 36 at lunchtime. How many more do they have to sell before the end of the day?

   A. 119 loaves
   B. 120 loaves
   C. 46 loaves
   D. 45 loaves

   3.OA.8 / 3.NBT.2

2. There are 12 tables at the cafe. Each table has 6 plates. If 23 plates on the tables need to be washed, how many plates are still clean?

   A. 41 plates   C. 50 plates
   B. 72 plates   D. 49 plates

   3.OA.8

3. Every week Hugo paints 4 more pictures for his studio. If he has painted 12 pictures already, how many more weeks will it take him to have painted 28 pictures?

   A. 4 weeks   C. 12 weeks
   B. 5 weeks   D. 16 weeks

   3.OA.8

4. Jeff recorded the hours he practiced piano each week before his concert. If this pattern continues, how many hours will he practice on Week 6?

Week 1	Week 2	Week 3	Week 4
6 hours	12 hours	18 hours	24 hours

   A. 30 hours
   B. 36 hours
   C. 42 hours
   D. 48 hours

   3.OA.9

5. Which pattern can be described as "times 3"?

   A. 3, 6, 9, 12
   B. 1, 3, 6, 12
   C. 1, 3, 9, 27
   D. 1, 3, 18, 27

   3.OA.9

6. Mr. Johnson has two dozen cookies and three dozen brownies. How many many sweet treats does he have altogether?

   A. 24 treats
   B. 36 treats
   C. 50 treats
   D. 60 treats

   3.OA.7 / 3.OA.8

Sometimes multiplication and addition have similar keywords like "more" or "in all". Ask yourself which operation makes the most since in each situation.

WEEK 8 : DAY 5

ASSESSMENT

1. The 3rd Grade is selling raffle tickets to raise money. They have already sold 89 tickets. Yesterday they sold 47 more. If the goal is to collect 200 tickets, how many more need to be sold?

   A. 136 tickets
   B. 111 tickets
   C. 64 tickets
   D. 65 tickets

   3.OA.8

2. The Farmer collected 234 eggs on Thursday and 375 eggs on Friday. Then he sold 412 eggs at the market on Saturday. How many does he have left?

   A. 609 eggs
   B. 196 eggs
   C. 198 eggs
   D. 197 eggs

   3.OA.8

3. The sports store sells baseballs in packs of 4. If they have 36 baseballs, how many packs do they have to sell?

   A. 10 packs
   B. 9 packs
   C. 8 packs
   D. 7 packs

   3.OA.6

4. Which of the following equations **would not** represent the picture below?

   A. 4 × 7 = 28
   B. 7 × 4 = 28
   C. 28 ÷ 4 = 7
   D. 28 ÷ 7 = 7

   3.OA.5

5. The library had 7 visitors on Monday, 14 on Tuesday, and 21 on Wednesday. If the pattern continues, how many visitors will the library have on Saturday?

   A. 28 visitors
   B. 35 visitors
   C. 42 visitors
   D. 49 visitors

   3.OA.9

6. Lily plants 7 new rose bushes each year. If she has 35 rose bushes already, how many total rose bushes will she have in 4 years?

   A. 28 rose bushes
   B. 63 rose bushes
   C. 42 rose bushes
   D. 49 rose bushes

   3.OA.8

DAY 6 Challenge question

Katey had 249 tokens for the arcade. After winning the challenge game, she was able to double her tokens. How many tokens does she have now?

3.OA.8

WEEK 9

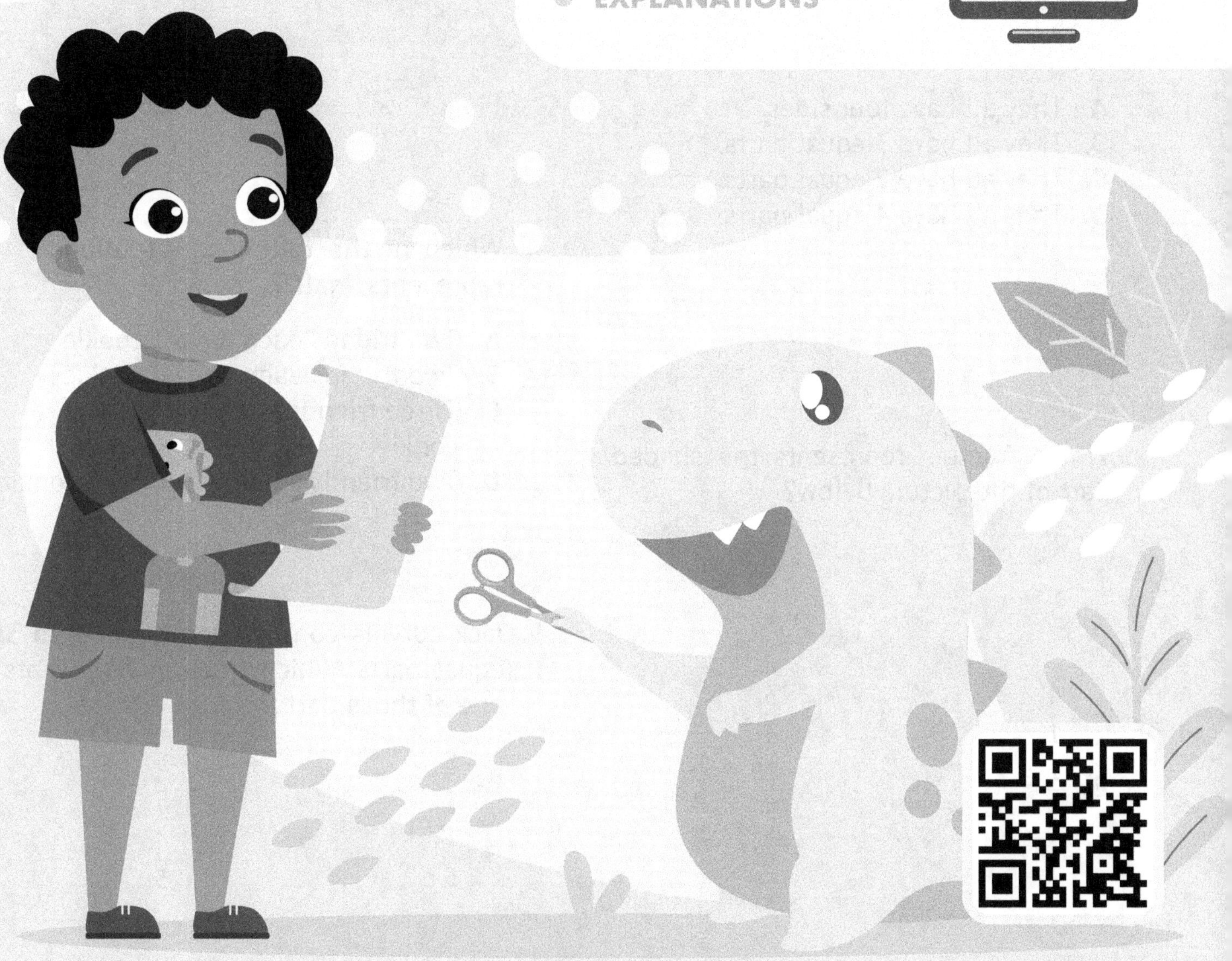

Week 9 is an exciting introduction to fractions. You will be asked to recognize equally partitioned shapes and name unit fractions. Problems will also include identifying fractions that are sums of unit fractions.

You can find detailed video explanations of each problem in the book by visiting: ArgoPrep.com

WEEK 9 : DAY 1

1. What do each of these shapes have in common?

   A. They all have four sides.
   B. They all have 3 equal parts.
   C. They all have 2 equal parts.
   D. They all have 4 equal parts.

   3.NF.1

2. Which fraction represents the shaded part of the picture below?

   A. $\dfrac{4}{1}$ C. $\dfrac{3}{4}$
   B. $\dfrac{1}{4}$ D. $\dfrac{1}{3}$

   3.NF.1

3. Sarah divides her brownie into 3 equal parts and eats one of the equal parts. What could her brownie look like?

   A.   C.
   B.   D.

   3.NF.1

4. Which of the following situations represents "half"?

   A. Two friends each have 1 cookie
   B. Two friends each have 2 cookies
   C. Three friends equally sharing 1 cookie
   D. Two friends equally sharing 1 cookie

   3.NF.1

5. Jack cut his construction paper into 5 equal parts. Which fraction represents one of those parts?

   A. $\dfrac{5}{1}$ C. $\dfrac{5}{5}$
   B. $\dfrac{1}{5}$ D. $\dfrac{4}{5}$

   3.NF.1

TIP of the DAY

When dividing something in "half," both parts have to be exactly the same size. Make sure that your "halves" look equal!

WEEK 9 : DAY 2

1. What is the name of the piece below that is *not shaded*?

   A. $\frac{1}{2}$ or one half   C. $\frac{1}{4}$ or one fourth

   B. $\frac{1}{4}$ or one half   D. $\frac{1}{2}$ or one fourth

   3.NF.1

2. Which of the following situations correctly represents $\frac{1}{6}$?

   A. 1 piece of paper cut equally into 6 pieces
   B. 6 pieces of paper cut equally into 6 pieces
   C. 6 pieces of paper cut equally into 10 pieces
   D. 10 pieces of paper cut equally into 6 pieces

   3.NF.1

3. Which of the following represents one-eighth?

   A. $\frac{8}{8}$ C. $\frac{8}{1}$

   B. $\frac{1}{8}$ D. $\frac{1}{1}$

   3.NF.1

4. Which picture below *would not* represent $\frac{1}{3}$?

   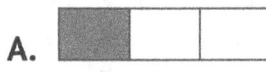

   A.   C.

   B.   D.

   3.NF.1

5. Which fraction is represented by the shaded portion of the picture below?

   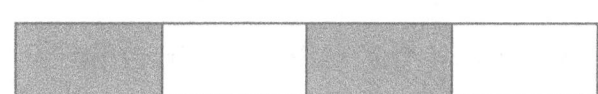

   A. $\frac{1}{4}$ C. $\frac{2}{2}$

   B. $\frac{2}{4}$ D. $\frac{4}{2}$

   3.NF.1

TIP of the DAY

Two halves can only be equal if they came from equal wholes. Think about it: half of a small pizza is not the same as half of a large pizza.

63

WEEK 9 : DAY 3

1. Which of the following pictures represents $\frac{2}{3}$?

   A. 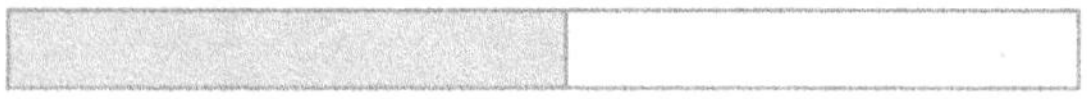
   B.
   C.
   D.

   3.NF.1

2. Lillian cut her pie into 8 equal pieces. She served 5 of the pieces. Which fraction represents how much of the cake she served?

   A. $\frac{8}{5}$ C. $\frac{1}{8}$
   B. $\frac{1}{5}$ D. $\frac{5}{8}$

   3.NF.1

3. Which of the following fractions represents two-sixths?

   A. $\frac{2}{2}$ C. $\frac{2}{6}$
   B. $\frac{6}{2}$ D. $\frac{6}{6}$

   3.NF.1

4. The picture below represents Hannah's garden. The unshaded part represents how much of the garden is roses. What fraction of Hannah's garden is roses?

   A. $\frac{2}{3}$ C. $\frac{3}{5}$
   B. $\frac{2}{5}$ D. $\frac{1}{5}$

   3.NF.1

5. Which of the following situations represents $\frac{1}{4}$?

   A. 4 friends share 4 cookies
   B. 2 friends share 2 cookies
   C. 2 friends share 1 cookie
   D. 4 friends share 1 cookie

   3.NF.1

6. Which fraction represents three-eighths?

   A. $\frac{8}{3}$ C. $\frac{1}{3}$
   B. $\frac{3}{8}$ D. $\frac{8}{8}$

   3.NF.1

TIP of the DAY

The denominator always represents how many equal parts are in a whole. If your whole is divided into 8 equal parts, one piece of your whole would be $\frac{1}{8}$.

WEEK 9 : DAY 4

1. Which fraction of the shape is shaded?

   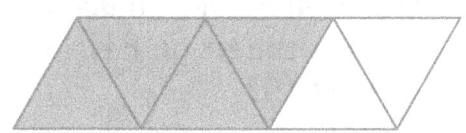

   A. $\frac{4}{2}$ C. $\frac{4}{4}$
   B. $\frac{1}{6}$ D. $\frac{4}{6}$

   3.NF.1

2. Kendall cut his cake into 8 pieces. Over the last week he has eaten 6 pieces. What fraction of his cake has he eaten?

   A. $\frac{8}{6}$ C. $\frac{6}{8}$
   B. $\frac{1}{6}$ D. $\frac{1}{8}$

   3.NF.1

3. Which of the following pictures represents three-fifths?

   3.NF.1

4. Which of the following is equal to $\frac{1}{4}$?

   A. one fourth
   B. four wholes
   C. four fourths
   D. two quarters

   3.NF.1

5. Melanie was drawing a map of her yard. The shaded part represents areas of grass. What fraction of her yard is grass?

   A. $\frac{3}{3}$ C. $\frac{3}{6}$
   B. $\frac{1}{4}$ D. $\frac{6}{3}$

   3.NF.1

TIP of the DAY

The numerator always represents how many pieces of the whole you have. If your whole is divided into 8 equal parts, and you have 2 pieces, your fraction would be $\frac{2}{8}$.

65

WEEK 9 : DAY 5

ASSESSMENT

1. Which picture below represents two-thirds?

   A. ▮▮▯▯▯
   B. ▮▮▮▯
   C. ▮▮▯▯
   D. ▮▮▮▮

   3.NF.1

2. Shelton has a garden that is divided into 8 equal parts. 5 of those parts are growing corn. Which fraction represents how much of his garden is growing corn?

   A. $\frac{5}{5}$ C. $\frac{8}{5}$
   B. $\frac{5}{8}$ D. $\frac{1}{8}$

   3.NF.1

3. There are only 35 cupcakes for the party. 5 cupcakes will be put on each table. How many tables can cupcakes be put on?

   A. 4 tables   C. 6 tables
   B. 5 tables   D. 7 tables

   3.OA.6 / 3.OA.7

4. Half of Joey's marble collection has 234 marbles. **About** how much does his whole marble collection have, rounded to the nearest 10?

   A. 468   C. 460
   B. 470   D. 500

   3.NBT.1 / 3.NBT.2 / 3.NF.1

5. The picture below represents Mr. Cho's flower patch. The unshaded part represents his daisies. What fraction of his flower patch is daisies?

   A. $\frac{2}{4}$ C. $\frac{2}{6}$
   B. $\frac{6}{2}$ D. $\frac{4}{6}$

   3.NF.1

6. Kady made 5 cakes. Each cake was divided equally into 12 pieces. How many pieces of cake does Kady have altogether?

   A. 65 pieces   C. 55 pieces
   B. 60 pieces   D. 50 pieces

   3.OA.1

DAY 6
Challenge question

Kaitlyn cut her pie into 8 equal pieces. Her family ate 3 pieces last night and 2 pieces tonight. What fraction of the cake has her family eaten?

3.NF.1

WEEK 10

VIDEO EXPLANATIONS

ARGOPREP.COM

The problems in Week 10 focus on placing fractions on a number line between 0 and 1. You will be asked to determine the numerator and denominator of a fraction given its location on a number line, as well as naming fractions that represent real-world situations.

You can find detailed video explanations of each problem in the book by visiting: ArgoPrep.com

WEEK 10 : DAY 1

1. Which fraction is represented by the star on the number line?

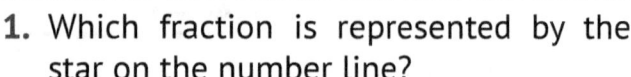

   A. $\frac{1}{3}$ C. $\frac{3}{2}$
   B. $\frac{2}{3}$ D. $\frac{1}{2}$

   3.NF.2

2. Which fraction is missing from the number line?

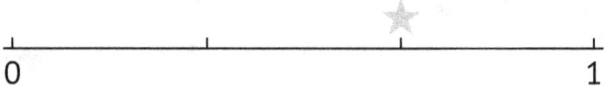

   A. $\frac{2}{5}$ C. $\frac{2}{3}$
   B. $\frac{2}{4}$ D. $\frac{2}{6}$

   3.NF.2

3. Shelley wants to put $\frac{4}{8}$ on a number line. How many equal parts should her number line have between 0 and 1?

   A. 4 equal parts   C. 8 equal parts
   B. 2 equal parts   D. 1 equal part

   3.NF.2

4. Which fraction represents one equal part of this number line?

   A. $\frac{1}{6}$ B. $\frac{1}{5}$ C. $\frac{1}{4}$ D. $\frac{1}{3}$

   3.NF.2

5. Which of the expressions below equals $\frac{2}{5}$?

   A. $\frac{1}{5} + \frac{1}{5}$ C. $\frac{1}{5} + 1$
   B. $\frac{5}{5} + 1$ D. $\frac{1}{5} + \frac{1}{5} + \frac{1}{5}$

   3.NF.2

6. Which fraction is represented by the star on the number line?

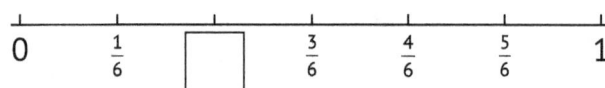

   A. $\frac{1}{6}$ or one-sixth
   B. $\frac{2}{6}$ or two-sixths
   C. $\frac{4}{8}$ or four-eighths
   D. $\frac{3}{8}$ or three-eighths

   3.NF.2

TIP of the DAY

When placing fractions on a number line, first make sure you know where "0" and "1" are. Any unit fraction (like $\frac{1}{2}$ or $\frac{1}{4}$) must be located between 0 and 1.

68

WEEK 10 : DAY 2

1. Simone wants to put her fraction, $\frac{3}{8}$, on a number line. How many equal parts does her number line need to have between 0 and 1?

   A. 3 equal parts   C. 5 equal parts
   B. 8 equal parts   D. 1 equal part

   3.NF.2

2. Which fractions are missing from the number line below?

   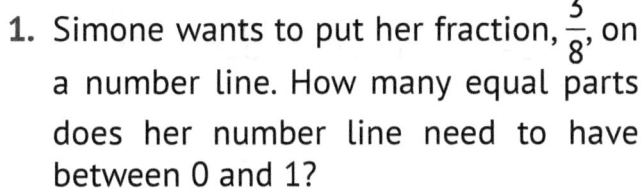

   A. $\frac{1}{8}, \frac{4}{8}$ and $\frac{7}{8}$ C. $\frac{1}{8}$ and $\frac{7}{8}$ only
   B. $\frac{1}{8}, \frac{4}{8}$ and $\frac{8}{8}$ D. $\frac{1}{8}$ and $\frac{4}{8}$ only

   3.NF.2

3. Which fraction is represented by the number line below?

   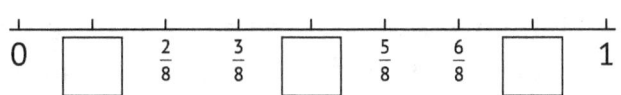

   A. one-fourth   C. three-fourths
   B. two-fourths   D. four-fourths

   3.NF.2

4. Which fraction is equal to one-eighth?

   A. $\frac{8}{1}$ C. $\frac{8}{8}$
   B. $\frac{1}{8}$ D. $\frac{1}{1}$

   3.NF.1

5. Which place on the number line is equal to the fraction represented in this picture:

    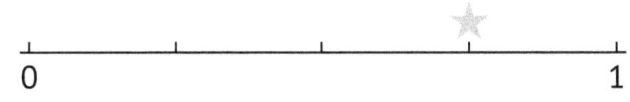

   A. $\frac{1}{4}$ C. $\frac{3}{4}$
   B. $\frac{2}{4}$ D. $\frac{4}{4}$ or 1 whole

   3.NF.2

6. Which of the following expressions equals $\frac{3}{4}$?

   A. $\frac{1}{3} + \frac{1}{3} + \frac{1}{3} + \frac{1}{3}$ C. $\frac{1}{4} + \frac{1}{3}$
   B. $\frac{1}{4} + \frac{1}{4}$ D. $\frac{1}{4} + \frac{1}{4} + \frac{1}{4}$

   3.NF.2

TIP of the DAY

Your number line should be divided into equal parts represented by your denominator. If the fraction is $\frac{1}{6}$, the denominator "6" shows that your number line should have 6 equal parts.

WEEK 10 : DAY 3

1. Jenny is running a marathon. The number line below represents how far Jenny has run so far. What fraction of the race has she completed?

   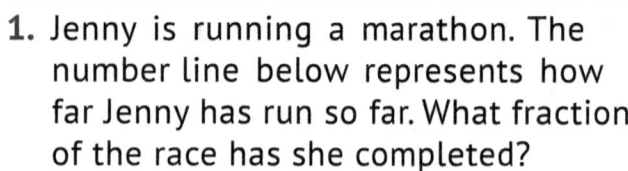

   A. $\frac{4}{4}$ of the race   C. $\frac{2}{6}$ of the race

   B. $\frac{4}{2}$ of the race   D. $\frac{4}{6}$ of the race

   3.NF.2

2. Which of the following is *not equal* to $\frac{6}{8}$?

   A. $\frac{1}{8} + \frac{1}{8} + \frac{1}{8} + \frac{1}{8} + \frac{1}{8} + \frac{1}{8}$

   B. $\frac{1}{8} + \frac{1}{8} + \frac{2}{8} + \frac{2}{8} + \frac{2}{8}$

   C. $\frac{2}{8} + \frac{2}{8} + \frac{2}{8}$

   D. $\frac{4}{8} + \frac{1}{8} + \frac{1}{8}$

   3.NF.2

3. Which of the following fractions represents one equal part on this number line?

   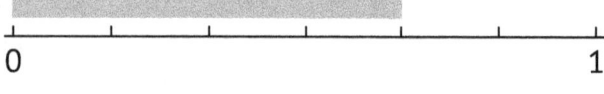

   A. one-eighth
   B. one-sixth
   C. one-fourth
   D. one-tenth

   3.NF.2

4. Julio made a cake and cut it into 8 equal pieces. His dad ate 2 pieces and his brother ate one piece. What fraction of Julio's cake has been eaten?

   A. $\frac{2}{8}$ C. $\frac{3}{8}$

   B. $\frac{1}{8}$ D. $\frac{5}{8}$

   3.NF.1

5. Which place on the number line is equal to three-fifths?

   ├──A.──B.──C.──D.──┤
   0   1

   3.NF.2

TIP of the DAY

The numerator shows you how far along the number line you should place your fraction. If you have the fraction $\frac{2}{5}$, you should place your fraction two "fifths" of the way between 0 and 1.

70

WEEK 10 : DAY 4

1. Which expression represents the number line below?

   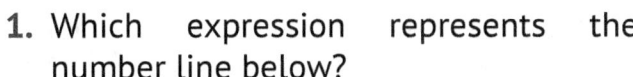
   0   1

   A. $\frac{1}{3} = \frac{1}{3}$ C. $\frac{1}{3} + \frac{1}{3} + \frac{1}{3} = \frac{2}{3}$

   B. $\frac{1}{3} + \frac{1}{3} = \frac{2}{3}$ D. $2 + \frac{1}{3} = \frac{2}{3}$

   3.NF.2

2. Which of the following statements is *false*?

   A. $\frac{3}{4}$ = 1 whole

   B. $\frac{4}{4}$ = 1 whole

   C. eight-eighths = 1 whole

   D. $\frac{1}{3} + \frac{1}{3} + \frac{1}{3}$ = 1 whole

   3.NF.2

3. Cathy has a piece of paper that she cut into 3 equal parts. She colors on two of the equal parts. What fraction of the paper has she *not* colored on?

   A. $\frac{1}{2}$ B. $\frac{1}{3}$ C. $\frac{2}{3}$ D. $\frac{3}{3}$

   3.NF.2

4. Which fractions are missing on the number line?

   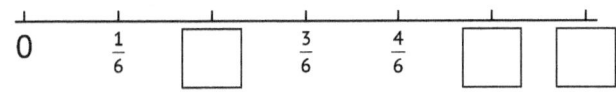
   0   $\frac{1}{6}$ ☐ $\frac{3}{6}$ $\frac{4}{6}$ ☐   ☐

   A. $\frac{2}{6}$ and $\frac{5}{6}$ only   C. $\frac{2}{6}, \frac{5}{6}$, and $\frac{7}{6}$

   B. $\frac{5}{6}$ and $\frac{7}{6}$ only   D. $\frac{2}{6}, \frac{5}{6}$, and $\frac{6}{6}$

   3.NF.2

5. Which equation correctly shows how to decompose $\frac{4}{6}$?

   A. $4 + \frac{1}{6} = \frac{4}{6}$

   B. $\frac{4}{6} + \frac{4}{6} + \frac{4}{6} + \frac{4}{6} = \frac{4}{6}$

   C. $\frac{1}{6} + \frac{1}{6} + \frac{1}{6} + \frac{1}{6} = \frac{4}{6}$

   D. $\frac{4}{6} + \frac{1}{6} = \frac{4}{6}$

   3.NF.2

6. Which of the following fractions *does not* equal one whole?

   A. four-fourths   C. five-sixths
   B. five-fifths   D. three-thirds

   3.NF.2

TIP of the DAY

If your numerator is larger than your denominator, your fraction will probably lie beyond "1" on the number line. Fractions like $\frac{6}{1}$ and $\frac{4}{2}$ are greater than "one whole."

WEEK 10 : DAY 5

ASSESSMENT

1. Which equation represents the number line below?

   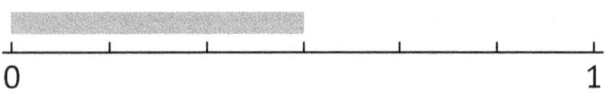

   A. $\frac{3}{6} + \frac{3}{6} = \frac{6}{6}$

   B. $\frac{1}{6} + \frac{1}{6} + \frac{2}{6} = \frac{4}{6}$

   C. $\frac{1}{6} + \frac{1}{6} + \frac{1}{6} = \frac{3}{6}$

   D. $\frac{1}{6} + \frac{3}{6} = \frac{3}{6}$

   3.NF.2

2. Which fractions are represented by the boxes on the number line below?

   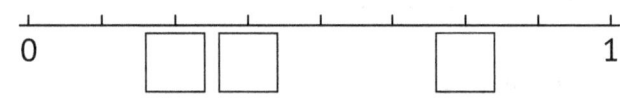

   A. $\frac{1}{8}, \frac{2}{8}$ and $\frac{6}{8}$

   B. $\frac{1}{8}, \frac{2}{8}$ and $\frac{5}{8}$

   C. $\frac{1}{8}, \frac{2}{8}$ and $\frac{6}{8}$

   D. $\frac{2}{8}, \frac{3}{8}$ and $\frac{5}{8}$

   3.NF.2

3. Which fraction represents the **shaded** part of the picture below?

   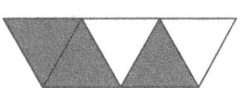

   A. $\frac{2}{3}$ B. $\frac{2}{5}$ C. $\frac{3}{5}$ D. $\frac{5}{5}$

   3.NF.1

4. Mr. Getty wants to give an equal amount of stickers to 9 students. He has 72 stickers. How many stickers will each student get?

   A. 6 stickers
   B. 7 stickers
   C. 8 stickers
   D. 9 stickers

   3.OA.6

5. Jamison has 202 baseball cards. Gerson has **twice** as many as Jamison. How many cards do they have altogether?

   A. 404
   B. 606
   C. 604
   D. 406

   3.NBT.2 / 3.OA.8

6. Which of the following is **not equal** to $\frac{4}{5}$?

   A. $\frac{1}{5} + \frac{2}{5}$

   B. $\frac{1}{5} + \frac{1}{5} + \frac{2}{5}$

   C. $\frac{1}{5} + \frac{1}{5} + \frac{1}{5} + \frac{1}{5}$

   D. $\frac{1}{5} + \frac{3}{5}$

   3.NF.2

DAY 6 Challenge question

Marcy is running a marathon. There are 8 equal sections of the marathon. By 8:00am she has run $\frac{2}{8}$ of the marathon. By 10:00am she has run $\frac{3}{8}$ more of the marathon. How much of the total marathon does she have left to run?

3.NF.2

WEEK 11

ARGOPREP.COM

VIDEO
EXPLANATIONS

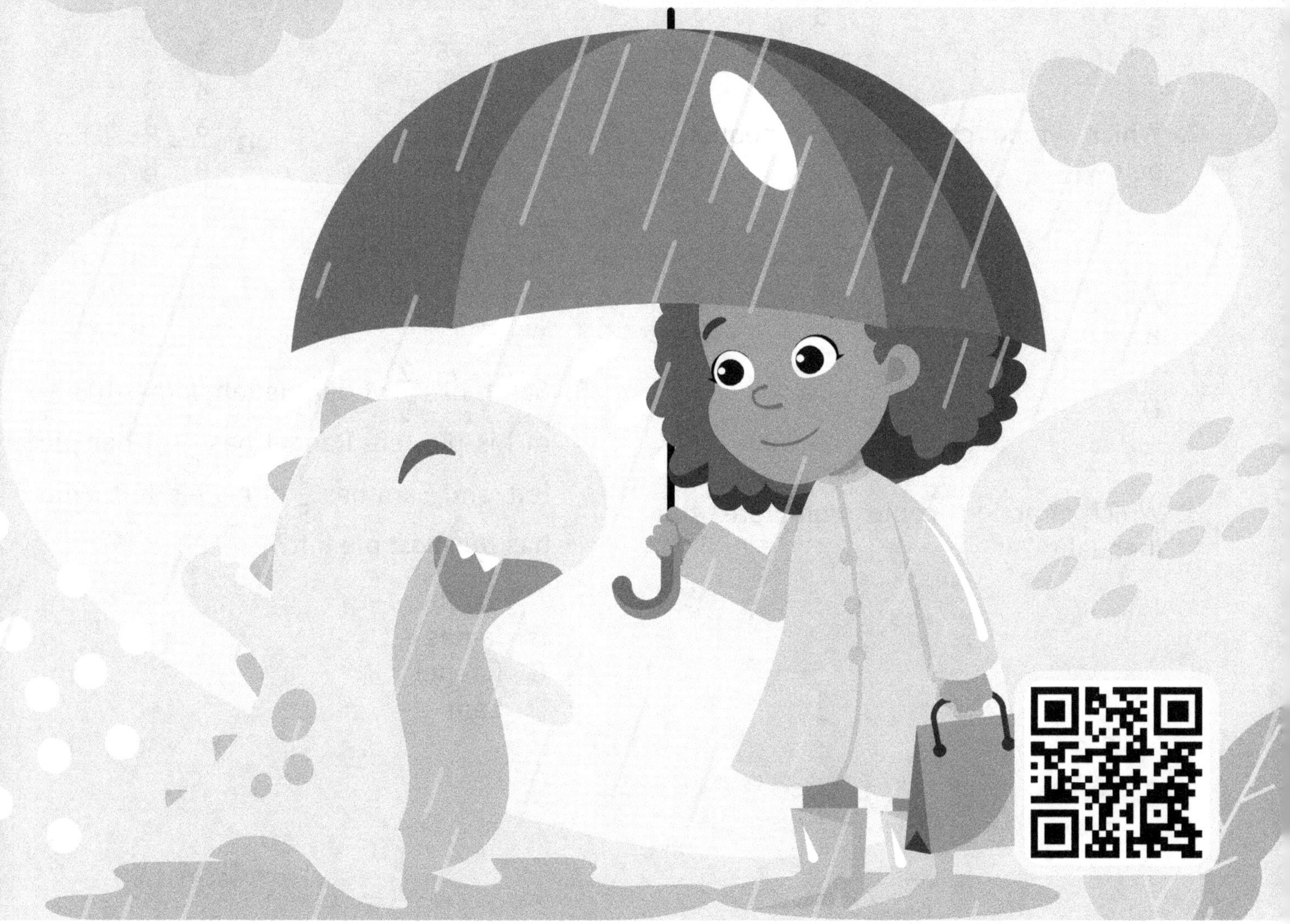

Week 11 is all about comparing and ordering fractions. You will use equally partitioned shapes and number lines to determine if two fractions are equivalent or not. You will also be asked to reason about the size of fractions based on their numerators and denominators.

You can find detailed video explanations of each problem in the book by visiting: ArgoPrep.com

WEEK 11 : DAY 1

1. Which of the following fractions is the *largest*?

   A. $\frac{1}{2}$ C. $\frac{1}{4}$

   B. $\frac{1}{3}$ D. $\frac{1}{5}$

   3.NF.3

2. Which symbol completes the inequality below?

   $\frac{2}{4} \square \frac{3}{4}$

   A. >
   B. <
   C. =
   D. +

   3.NF.3

3. Which fraction could complete the inequality?

   $\square > \frac{1}{4}$

   A. $\frac{1}{6}$ C. $\frac{1}{2}$

   B. $\frac{1}{5}$ D. $\frac{1}{10}$

   3.NF.3

4. Which inequality does the following picture represent?

   A. $\frac{1}{4} = \frac{6}{8}$ C. $\frac{3}{4} > \frac{6}{8}$

   B. $\frac{3}{4} < \frac{6}{8}$ D. $\frac{3}{4} = \frac{6}{8}$

   3.NF.3

5. Sarah has $\frac{2}{5}$ of her pie left, James has $\frac{4}{5}$ of his pie left, Raquel has $\frac{1}{5}$ of her pie left, and Sam has $\frac{3}{5}$ of his pie left. Who has *the most* pie left?

   A. Sarah
   B. James
   C. Raquel
   D. Sam

   3.NF.3

TIP of the DAY: When comparing two fractions, use the denominators to think about the size of each piece. For example, $\frac{2}{4}$ would be more than $\frac{2}{8}$ because a fourth is bigger than an eighth.

WEEK 11 : DAY 2

1. Which of the inequalities is ***true*** based on the picture below?

A. $\frac{4}{5} < \frac{3}{4}$

B. $\frac{4}{5} > \frac{3}{4}$

C. $\frac{4}{5} = \frac{3}{4}$

D. $\frac{3}{4} > \frac{4}{5}$

3.NF.3

2. Which of the following fractions is the ***largest***?

$$\frac{4}{5}, \frac{4}{8}, \frac{4}{6}$$

A. $\frac{4}{8}$ is the largest

B. $\frac{4}{5}$ is the largest

C. $\frac{4}{6}$ is the largest

D. They are all equal

3.NF.3

3. Which symbol would make this inequality ***true***?

$$\frac{1}{3} \square \frac{1}{8}$$

A. <   B. >   C. =   D. +

3.NF.3

4. Jared has $\frac{3}{12}$ of a cake left. Jason has $\frac{3}{4}$ of a cake left. Who has more?

A. Jared has more because he has 12 equal pieces left.

B. Jared has more because he has 3 out of 12 equal pieces left.

C. Jason has more because he has 3 out of 4 equal pieces left.

D. They both have the same amount left.

3.NF.3

5. Which of the following fractions is ***larger*** than $\frac{5}{8}$?

A. $\frac{1}{8}$ B. $\frac{2}{8}$ C. $\frac{4}{8}$ D. $\frac{5}{6}$

3.NF.3

6. Which fraction is ***less than*** the fraction represented on the number line below?

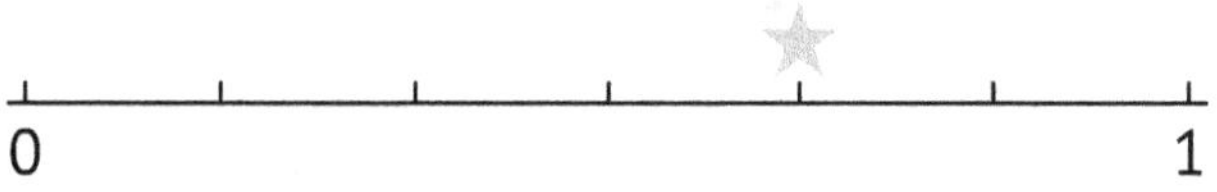

A. $\frac{4}{8}$ B. $\frac{4}{5}$ C. $\frac{5}{6}$ D. $\frac{6}{6}$

3.NF.1 / 3.NF.3

TIP of the DAY

If two fractions have the same denominator, just compare the numerators to see which one is bigger. You can tell that $\frac{4}{6}$ is bigger than $\frac{2}{6}$ because it has more "sixths".

WEEK 11 : DAY 3

1. Which symbol would make the inequality below *true*?

   $\frac{3}{3}$ ☐ 1 whole

   A. < B. > C. = D. +

   3.NF.3

2. Put the following fractions in order, from *least to greatest*.

   $\frac{3}{8}, \frac{3}{5}, \frac{3}{4}, \frac{3}{6}$

   A. $\frac{3}{8}, \frac{3}{6}, \frac{3}{5}, \frac{3}{4}$ C. $\frac{3}{5}, \frac{3}{4}, \frac{3}{8}, \frac{3}{6}$

   B. $\frac{3}{6}, \frac{3}{5}, \frac{3}{4}, \frac{3}{8}$ D. $\frac{3}{4}, \frac{3}{5}, \frac{3}{6}, \frac{3}{8}$

   3.NF.3

3. Which inequality is represented by the picture below?

   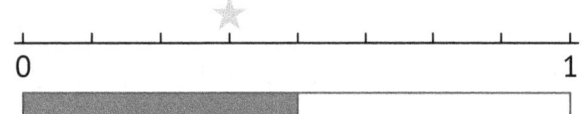

   A. $\frac{3}{8} = \frac{1}{2}$ C. $\frac{3}{8} < \frac{1}{2}$

   B. $\frac{1}{2} < \frac{3}{8}$ D. $\frac{3}{8} > \frac{1}{2}$

   3.NF.3

4. This week it rained $\frac{1}{4}$ inch on Tuesday, $\frac{1}{3}$ inch on Wednesday, $\frac{1}{6}$ inch on Thursday, and $\frac{1}{8}$ inch on Friday. Which day did it rain the *least*?

   A. Tuesday C. Thursday
   B. Wednesday D. Friday

   3.NF.3

5. Which of the following fractions is the *greatest*?

   A. $\frac{3}{4}$ C. $\frac{3}{6}$

   B. $\frac{3}{8}$ D. $\frac{3}{5}$

   3.NF.3

6. Which of the following fractions is the *least*?

   A. $\frac{1}{2}$ C. $\frac{1}{4}$

   B. $\frac{1}{6}$ D. $\frac{1}{5}$

   3.NF.3

TIP of the DAY

If your numerator and denominator are the same size, you have one whole! Therefore, $\frac{3}{3}$ = 1 whole just like $\frac{6}{6}$ = 1 whole.

WEEK 11 : DAY 4

1. Which inequality is represented by the picture below?

   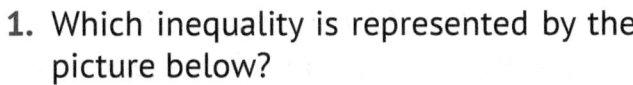

   A. $\dfrac{4}{4} < \dfrac{2}{2} < \dfrac{3}{3}$ C. $\dfrac{2}{2} = \dfrac{3}{3} = \dfrac{4}{4}$

   B. $\dfrac{2}{2} > \dfrac{3}{3} > \dfrac{4}{4}$ D. $\dfrac{3}{3} < \dfrac{2}{2} > \dfrac{4}{4}$

   3.NF.3

2. Which symbol would make the following inequality *true*?

   $\dfrac{2}{3} \square \dfrac{2}{8}$

   A. <   B. >   C. =   D. +

   3.NF.3

3. Which inequality represents the picture below?

   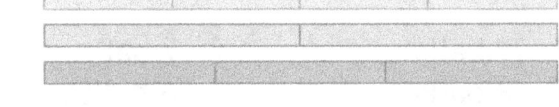

   A. $\dfrac{4}{6} < \dfrac{2}{3}$ C. $\dfrac{2}{3} = \dfrac{4}{6}$

   B. $\dfrac{4}{6} > \dfrac{2}{3}$ D. $\dfrac{2}{3} < \dfrac{4}{6}$

   3.NF.3

4. Which of the following fractions is the *least*?

   A. $\dfrac{2}{5}$ C. $\dfrac{2}{6}$

   B. $\dfrac{2}{4}$ D. $\dfrac{2}{8}$

   3.NF.3

5. Jamill made a cake. He cut it into 8 equal slices. He has not eaten any of the cake. Which fraction *does not* represent how much cake Jamill has left?

   A. $\dfrac{1}{8}$ C. one whole

   B. eight-eighths   D. $\dfrac{8}{8}$

   3.NF.3

6. Which fraction could complete the inequality below?

   $\dfrac{3}{5} < \square$

   A. $\dfrac{3}{8}$ C. $\dfrac{3}{6}$

   B. $\dfrac{3}{4}$ D. $\dfrac{3}{10}$

   3.NF.1 / 3.NF.3

TIP of the DAY

When writing whole numbers as a fraction, just put the whole number over 1. For example, $\dfrac{5}{1}$ is like saying "5 wholes."

WEEK 11 : DAY 5

ASSESSMENT

1. Which fraction is **less than** the fraction represented on the number line below?

   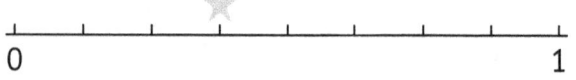

   A. $\dfrac{4}{8}$ C. $\dfrac{5}{8}$

   B. $\dfrac{6}{8}$ D. $\dfrac{2}{8}$

   3.NF.1 / 3.NF.3

2. Haley started with 249 beads, and then bought 150 more. If she **doubles** her collection, how many beads will she have?

   A. 399   C. 798
   B. 400   D. 800

   3.NBT.2 / 3.OA.8

3. Put the following fractions in order, from **least to greatest**.

   $$\dfrac{1}{6}, \dfrac{1}{8}, \dfrac{1}{5}, \dfrac{1}{2}$$

   A. $\dfrac{1}{2}, \dfrac{1}{5}, \dfrac{1}{8}, \dfrac{1}{6}$ C. $\dfrac{1}{8}, \dfrac{1}{6}, \dfrac{1}{5}, \dfrac{1}{2}$

   B. $\dfrac{1}{2}, \dfrac{1}{5}, \dfrac{1}{6}, \dfrac{1}{8}$ D. $\dfrac{1}{8}, \dfrac{1}{2}, \dfrac{1}{5}, \dfrac{1}{6}$

   3.NF.3

4. Jermaine has 45 basketballs. He wants to put them equally into 5 baskets. How many balls will be in each basket?

   A. 9 balls   C. 7 balls
   B. 8 balls   D. 6 balls

   3.OA.6 / 3.OA.7

5. Which of the inequalities is **true** based on the picture?

   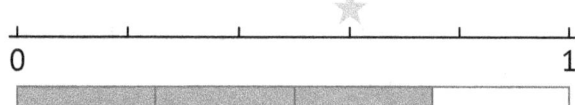

   A. $\dfrac{3}{5} = \dfrac{3}{4}$ C. $\dfrac{3}{5} > \dfrac{3}{4}$

   B. $\dfrac{3}{5} < \dfrac{3}{4}$ D. $\dfrac{3}{4} < \dfrac{3}{5}$

   3.NF.1 / 3.NF.3

6. Which of the following inequalities is **true**?

   A. $\dfrac{1}{3} + \dfrac{1}{3} < \dfrac{2}{4}$ C. $\dfrac{1}{5} + \dfrac{1}{5} > \dfrac{3}{5}$

   B. $\dfrac{1}{4} + \dfrac{1}{4} + \dfrac{1}{4} < \dfrac{3}{4}$ D. $\dfrac{1}{6} + \dfrac{1}{6} + \dfrac{1}{6} < \dfrac{4}{6}$

   3.NF.2 / 3.NF.3

DAY 6
Challenge question

Sandra cut her cake into 4 pieces and ate 2. Jack cut his cake into 5 pieces and ate 3. Who ate more cake?

3.NF.3

78

WEEK 12

ARGOPREP.COM

VIDEO
EXPLANATIONS

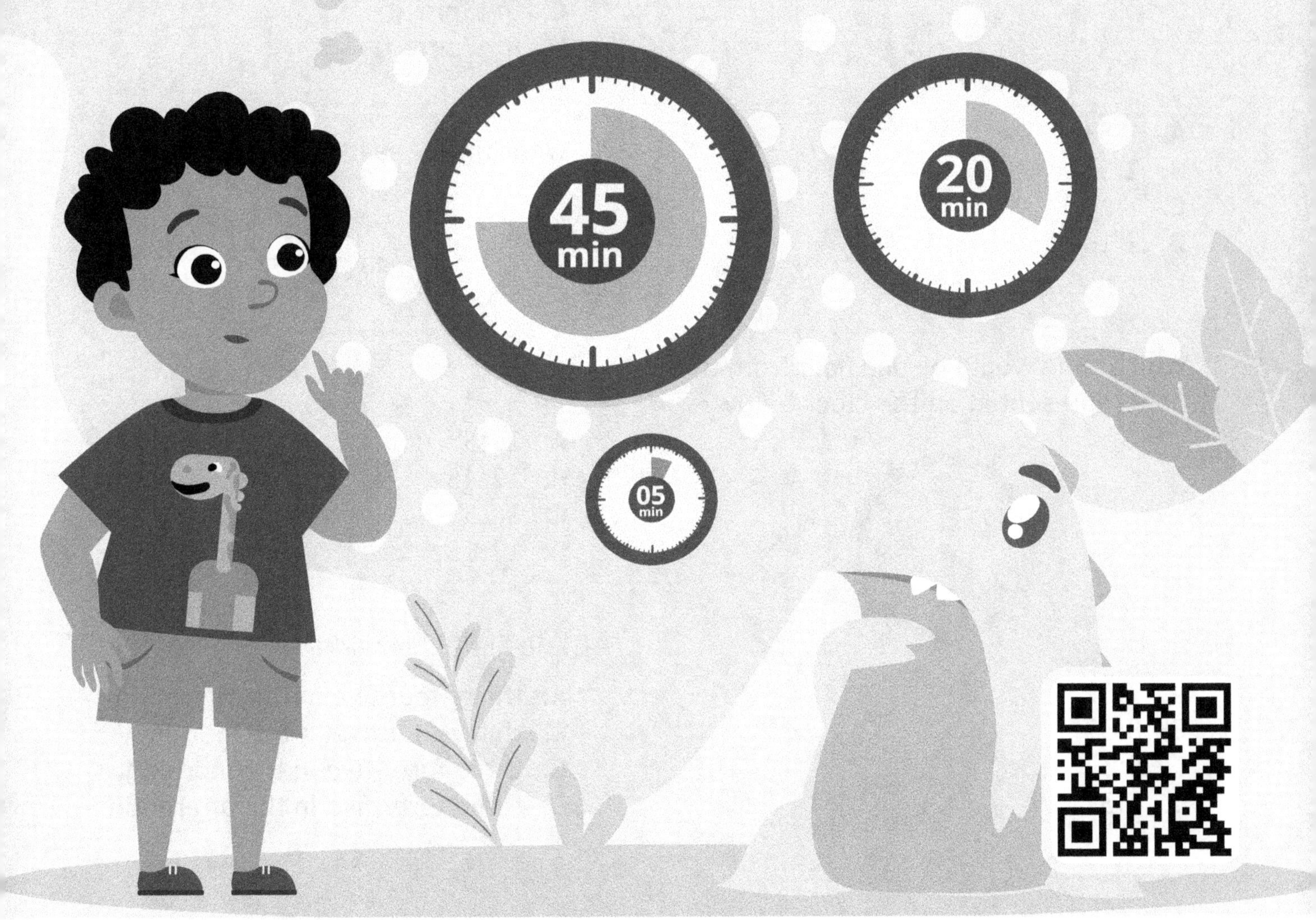

Time is the main focus of Week 12. Expressions of time like "half past" and "quarter till" are used in everyday conversation, and are important to practice. This week you will also solve problems including elapsed time, another real-world skill.

You can find detailed video explanations of each problem in the book by visiting: ArgoPrep.com

WEEK 12 : DAY 1

1. Which time is represented on the clock below?

   A. 1:53
   B. 2:53
   C. 1:10
   D. 2:10

   3.MD.1

2. Which time would be **one hour** from the time represented on the clock below?

   A. 7:32
   B. 8:32
   C. 6:37
   D. 7:37

   3.MD.1

3. Jim is going to the movies in 2 hours. It is now 4:45pm. What time is Jim going to the movies?

   A. 2:45pm
   B. 4:47pm
   C. 6:45pm
   D. 6:47pm

   3.MD.1

4. What time was it 15 minutes *ago*?

   A. 1:45
   B. 12:45
   C. 1:15
   D. 12:15

   3.MD.1

5. Which time is represented by 3:45pm?

   A. thirty-four five in the afternoon
   B. thirty-four five in the morning
   C. three forty-five in the morning
   D. three forty-five in the afternoon

   3.MD.1

TIP of the DAY

When reading a clock, remember that the short hand represents hours and the long hand represents minutes.

WEEK 12 : DAY 2

1. Which time is represented by 6:15pm?

   A. half-past 6 o'clock
   B. quarter-till 6 o'clock
   C. quarter-past 6'oclock
   D. half-till 6 o'clock

   3.MD.1

2. Jeanine's piano lesson is forty-five minutes long. It starts at 4 o'clock in the afternoon. What time will she finish?

   A. 4:45pm
   B. 5:45pm
   C. 4:15pm
   D. 5:15pm

   3.MD.1

3. Which time is represented by the clock below?

   A. 10:35pm   C. 7:55pm
   B. 11:35pm   D. 6:55pm

   3.MD.1

4. Mr. Hill is going to ring the bell at a quarter till four in the afternoon. What time will he ring the bell?

   A. 4:15pm
   B. 3:45pm
   C. 4:15am
   D. 3:45am

   3.MD.1

5. What time will it be in two hours?

   A. 1:42pm
   B. 2:42pm
   C. 3:42pm
   D. 4:42pm

   3.MD.1

TIP of the DAY

In telling time, "half past" means 30 minutes after the hour and "quarter past" means 15 minutes after the hour.

WEEK 12 : DAY 3

1. How much time has passed between the two clocks represented below?

   A. 1 hour and 5 minutes
   B. 2 hours and 5 minutes
   C. 1 hour and 15 minutes
   D. 2 hours and 15 minutes

   3.MD.1

2. Janell will go to the dentist in 1 hour and 30 minutes. It is now 2:50pm. What time will Janell go to the dentist?

   A. 3:50pm   C. 4:20pm
   B. 4:50pm   D. 3:20pm

   3.MD.1

3. The clock below represents the time now. What time will it be in two and a half hours?

   A. 1:50pm
   B. 12:50pm
   C. 1:34pm
   D. 12:34pm

   3.MD.1

4. What time is represented by half past twelve in the afternoon?

   A. 11:30am
   B. 12:30am
   C. 11:30pm
   D. 12:30pm

   3.MD.1

5. Mrs. Hernandez needs to meet her daughter at the airport at 6:00pm. It takes 50 minutes to drive to the airport. What time should Mrs. Hernandez leave for the airport?

   A. 6:50pm
   B. 6:10pm
   C. 5:10pm
   D. 5:50pm

   3.MD.1

6. What time is represented by 7:43am?

   A. seventy-four three in the morning
   B. seventy-four three in the afternoon
   C. seven forty-three in the afternoon
   D. seven forty-three in the morning

   3.MD.1

TIP of the DAY

Elapsed time means how much time has past from a given start time. To figure out the elapsed time, count the hours and minutes that have past from your start time.

82

WEEK 12 : DAY 4

1. The clock below represents what time Dina left for the beach. She arrived at 6:45pm. How long did it take Dina to drive to the beach?

   A. 2 hours and 30 minutes
   B. 3 hours and 30 minutes
   C. 2 hours and 15 minutes
   D. 3 hours and 15 minutes

   3.MD.1

2. What is the elapsed time between 12:34pm and 2:00pm?

   A. two hours and 26 minutes
   B. two hours and 36 minutes
   C. one hour and 26 minutes
   D. one hour and 36 minutes

   3.MD.1

3. Julia has ballet practice at 5:30pm. Her practice will last one hour and fifteen minutes. What time will Julia be finished with ballet practice?

   A. 5:45pm   C. 6:15pm
   B. 6:45pm   D. 6:00pm

   3.MD.1

4. What time is represented by quarter till eleven in the morning?

   A. 11:15pm
   B. 10:45pm
   C. 11:15am
   D. 10:45am

   3.MD.1

5. What is the elapsed time between the two times represented on the clocks below?

   A. 4 hours and 5 minutes
   B. 3 hours and 15 minutes
   C. 4 hours and 5 minutes
   D. 3 hours and 5 minutes

   3.MD.1

6. Which time is represented by 9:15am?

   A. quarter till 9 at night
   B. quarter past 9 at night
   C. quarter past 9 in the morning
   D. quarter till 9 in the morning

   3.MD.1

TIP of the DAY

When telling time, if the hour hand has not yet past the digit on the clock, it is still the previous hour. For example, even if the hour hand is close to the "8," but not past it, it's still within the 7 o'clock hour.

WEEK 12 : DAY 5

ASSESSMENT

1. The clock below represents when Simone arrived at the museum. She left the museum at 3:35pm. How much time did Simone spend at the museum?

   A. 1 hour and 35 minutes
   B. 1 hour and 45 minutes
   C. 35 minutes
   D. 45 minutes

   3.MD.1

2. Collin finished baseball practice at 7:00pm. If his practice was an hour and 25 minutes long, what time did his practice start?

   A. 6:35pm   C. 5:35pm
   B. 7:25pm   D. 5:25pm

   3.MD.1

3. Mr. Bates gave his students 17 minutes to complete each of four activity stations. *About* how much time did Mr. Bates give his students for all four of the stations?

   A. 68 minutes   C. 60 minutes
   B. 70 minutes   D. 80 minutes

   3.NBT.1

4. The Third Grade started math at 1:00pm. Math lasted 1 hour and 15 minutes, and then literacy lasted 1 hours and 40 minutes. What time did they finish literacy?

   A. 2:15pm   C. 3:15pm
   B. 2:55pm   D. 3:55pm

   3.MD.1

5. Haley has 142 marbles, Jay has 174 marbles, and Julius has **twice** as many marbles as Haley. How many marbles do they have altogether?

   A. 316   C. 600
   B. 458   D. 658

   3.NBT.2

6. What time will it be 2 hours and 15 minutes from the time on the clock below?

   A. 1:00
   B. 1:15
   C. 2:00
   D. 2:15

   3.MD.1

DAY 6 Challenge question

Mr. Allen starts exercising at 1:30pm. He runs for 45 minutes, swims for 35 minutes, and bikes for an hour. What time does Mr. Allen finish exercising?

3.MD.1

WEEK 13

ARGOPREP.COM

VIDEO EXPLANATIONS

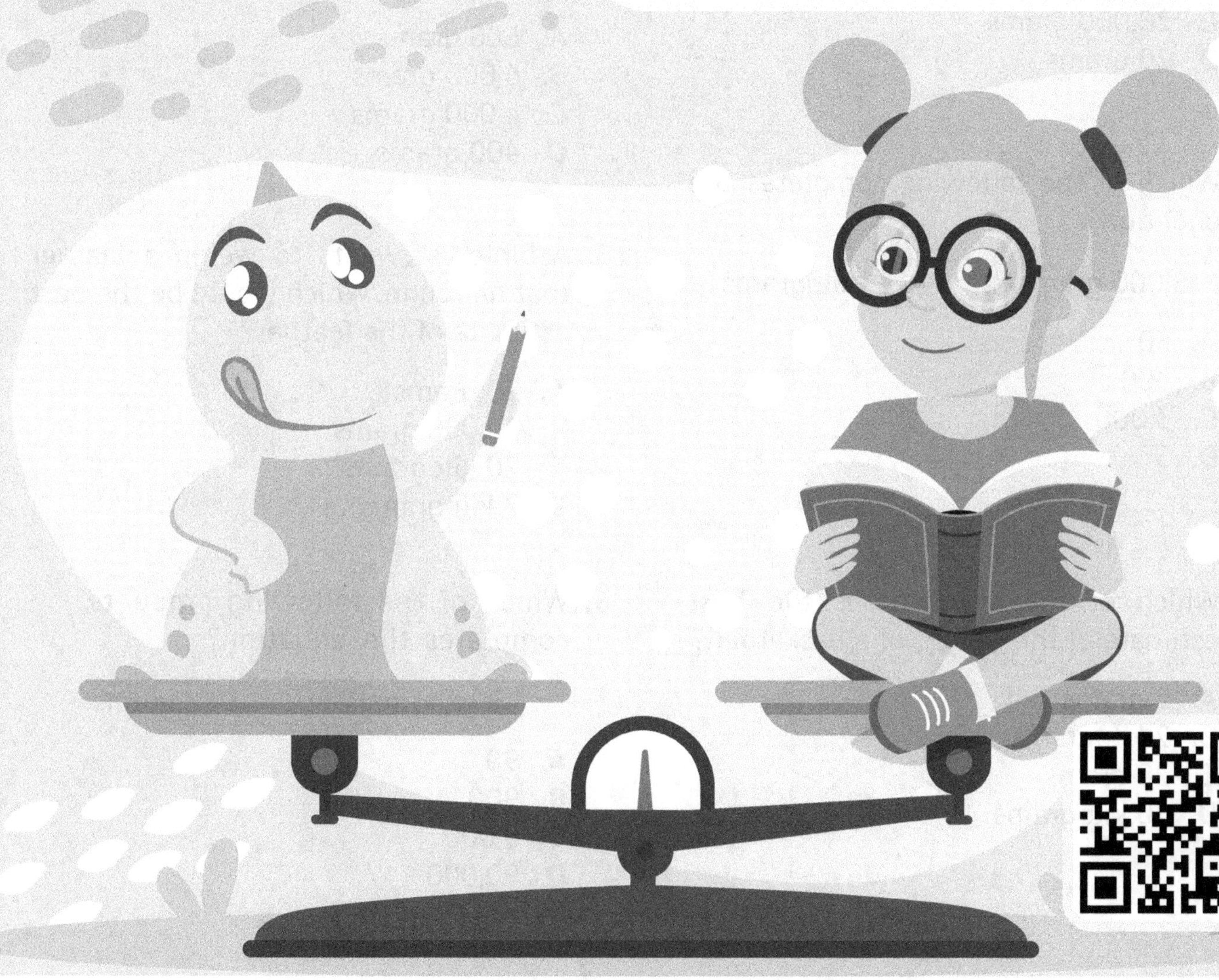

Measurement is the name of the game in Week 13. You will measure capacity using liters and milliliters, and you will measure weight, or mass, using kilograms and grams. Converting and estimating will be an important part of this week.

You can find detailed video explanations of each problem in the book by visiting: ArgoPrep.com

WEEK 13 : DAY 1

1. If a bucket weighs about 2 kilograms, how many **grams** does the bucket weigh?

   A. 200 grams
   B. 2,000 grams
   C. 20,000 grams
   D. 20 grams

   3.MD.2

2. Which of the following completes the equation?

   3,000 grams = ☐ kilograms

   A. 30
   B. 300
   C. 3,000
   D. 3

   3.MD.2

3. Which of the following is the best estimate of the weight of a basketball?

   A. 2 grams
   B. 2 kilograms
   C. 20 grams
   D. 20 kilograms

   3.MD.2

4. Look at the scale below. Which amount best fills in the missing number?

   | 600g | ? | | 1kg |

   A. 600 grams
   B. 6,000 grams
   C. 4,000 grams
   D. 400 grams

   3.MD.2 / 3.NBT.2

5. A biologist wants to weigh a feather that he found. Which would be the best estimate of the feather?

   A. 20 grams
   B. 20,000 grams
   C. 20 kilograms
   D. 2 kilograms

   3.MD.2

6. Which of the following amounts completes the equation?

   9 kilograms = ☐ grams

   A. 90
   B. 900
   C. 9,000
   D. 90,000

   3.MD.2

TIP of the DAY: When measuring weight, one kilogram is equal to 1,000 grams. Think of a gram like the weight of a paperclip, and a kilogram like the weight of a book.

WEEK 13 : DAY 2

1. Which of the following best completes the equation?

    2,000 mL = ☐ L

    A. 2
    B. 20
    C. 200
    D. 22

    3.MD.2

2. Alan has 2 containers that each have 2 liters of water in them. How many *milliliters* of water does Alan have altogether?

    A. 4 mL
    B. 40 mL
    C. 400 mL
    D. 4,000 mL

    3.MD.2 / 3.OA.8

3. Which symbol makes the following inequality *true*?

    5 liters ☐ 600 mL

    A. <
    B. >
    C. =
    D. +

    3.MD.2

4. The picture below shows one of Rhett's boxes of cds. If Rhett has 6 boxes just like this, how much do the boxes weigh altogether?

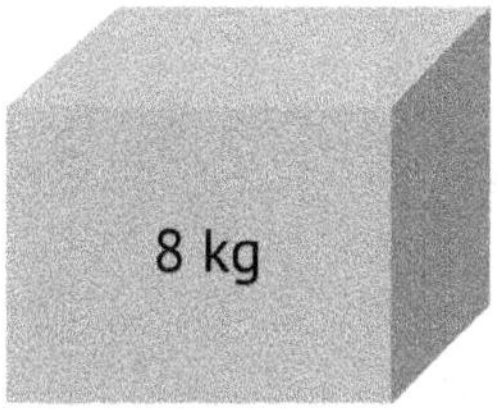

    8 kg

    A. 42 kg
    B. 40 kg
    C. 48 kg
    D. 56 kg

    3.MD.2 / 3.OA.6

5. Monique has two bags of sand that *each* weigh 4,000 grams. How many kilograms of sand does she have?

    A. 4 kilograms
    B. 8 kilograms
    C. 40 kilograms
    D. 80 kilograms

    3.MD.2

6. Which of the following could make the inequality below *true*?

    4,000 grams = ☐ kilograms

    A. 400
    B. 44
    C. 40
    D. 4

    3.MD.2

TIP of the DAY

When measuring capacity, 1,000 milliliters is equal to 1 liter. Since a liter is about the capacity of a gallon, you can picture 1,000 small drops of water making up one liter of water.

87

WEEK 13 : DAY 3

1. Which of the following would be the best estimate when measuring a small cup of milk?

   A. 40 kilograms
   B. 4,000 grams
   C. 40 liters
   D. 400 milliliters

   3.MD.2

2. Sam has three boxes that each have 3 kg worth of books in them. How many **grams** do the three boxes hold altogether?

   A. 6 grams
   B. 9 grams
   C. 6,000 grams
   D. 9,000 grams

   3.MD.2

3. If the two containers below are equal, how much does the second container hold?

   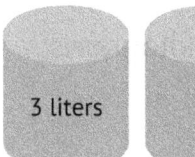

   A. 30 milliliters
   B. 300 milliliters
   C. 3 milliliters
   D. 3,000 milliliters

   3.MD.2

4. A farmer wants to weigh the watermelon that he just grew. What is the best estimate for the measurement of the watermelon?

   A. 90 grams
   B. 9 kilograms
   C. 90 milliliters
   D. 9 liters

   3.MD.2 / 3.NBT.2

5. Which of the following amounts could make the inequality **true**?

   6,000 grams > ☐ kilograms

   A. 5
   B. 6
   C. 7
   D. 8

   3.MD.2

6. The pet store owner has a bucket that holds 5 liters. If he wants to fill up a 25 liter fish tank, how many times will he have to fill up the bucket?

   A. 7 times
   B. 6 times
   C. 5 times
   D. 4 times

   3.MD.2 / 3.OA.7

TIP of the DAY: Capacity is usually best used to describe liquids, as it measures how much a container can hold. Weight is usually best used to describe solids, as it measures how heavy something is.

WEEK 13 : DAY 4

1. Look at the scale below. Which amount fills in the missing number?

   A. 387 grams
   B. 613 grams
   C. 614 grams
   D. 1,387 grams

   3.MD.2 / 3.NBT.2

2. Lea has 2 bags of soil. Each bag weighs 4 kilograms. How many **grams** of soil does Lea have altogether?

   A. 400 grams
   B. 4,000 grams
   C. 800 grams
   D. 8,000 grams

   3.MD.2

3. Three containers each hold 12 liters. How many liters do they hold altogether?

   A. 12 liters
   B. 24 liters
   C. 36 liters
   D. 48 liters

   3.MD.2 / 3.OA.1

4. The picture below represents one bucket of bricks.

   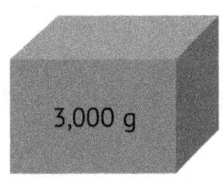

   How many **kilograms** of bricks does the bucket represent?

   A. 3 kg
   B. 30 kg
   C. 300 kg
   D. 3,000 kg

   3.MD.2

5. Emilio wants to weigh his soccer ball. What is the best estimate for measuring his soccer ball?

   A. 4 liters
   B. 4 kilograms
   C. 40 milliliters
   D. 40 grams

   3.MD.2

6. Which symbol would make the inequality **true**?

   4 kilograms ☐ 7,000 grams

   A. <
   B. >
   C. =
   D. +

   3.MD.2

TIP of the DAY

When trying to estimate how much a container can hold (capacity) or how heavy something is (weight), try to compare it to another object. If a book is about a kilogram, then a photo album is probably about a kilogram, too!

WEEK 13 : DAY 5

ASSESSMENT

1. The box below holds 4 kilograms. How many **grams** will two boxes hold?

   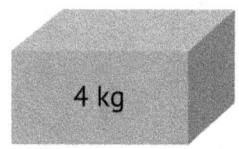

   A. 4,000 grams C. 400 grams
   B. 8,000 grams D. 800 grams

   3.MD.2

2. Charlotte has three boxes of old movies.

   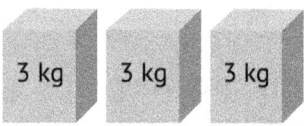

   How many **grams** do her movies weigh altogether?

   A. 9 grams   C. 900 grams
   B. 90 grams   D. 9,000 grams

   3.MD.2

3. There are 27 kilograms of stones in the workshop. If the stones are stored in bins of 3 kilograms each, how many bins are used to store the stones?

   A. 7 bins   C. 9 bins
   B. 8 bins   D. 10 bins

   3.MD.2 / 3.OA.7

4. Jeffrey has 2 liters of cola. Samuel has 3 liters of cola. How many **milliliters** of cola do they have altogether?

   A. 600 mL
   B. 6,000 mL
   C. 500 mL
   D. 5,000 mL

   3.MD.2

5. Mr. Tate has 438 grams of red marbles and 389 grams of blue marbles. **About** how many grams of marbles does he have altogether, rounded to the nearest 10?

   A. 830
   B. 820
   C. 827
   D. 828

   3.MD.2 / 3.NBT.1

6. Look at the scale below. Which amount best fills in the missing number?

   A. 540 grams   C. 460 grams
   B. 1,000 grams D. 440 grams

   3.MD.2 / 3.NBT.2

DAY 6
Challenge question

Helena has 3 liters of juice. Steve has twice as much as Helena. How many **milliliters** of juice do they have altogether?

3.MD.2

WEEK 14

VIDEO EXPLANATIONS → ARGOPREP.COM

Week 14 is all about graphs. Bar graphs and pictographs will allow you to show your understanding of collecting, interpreting, and making decisions about data. Don't forget to practice collecting and organizing your own data in a bar graph or pictograph!

You can find detailed video explanations of each problem in the book by visiting: ArgoPrep.com

WEEK 14 : DAY 1

Use the following bar graph to answer questions 1-6.

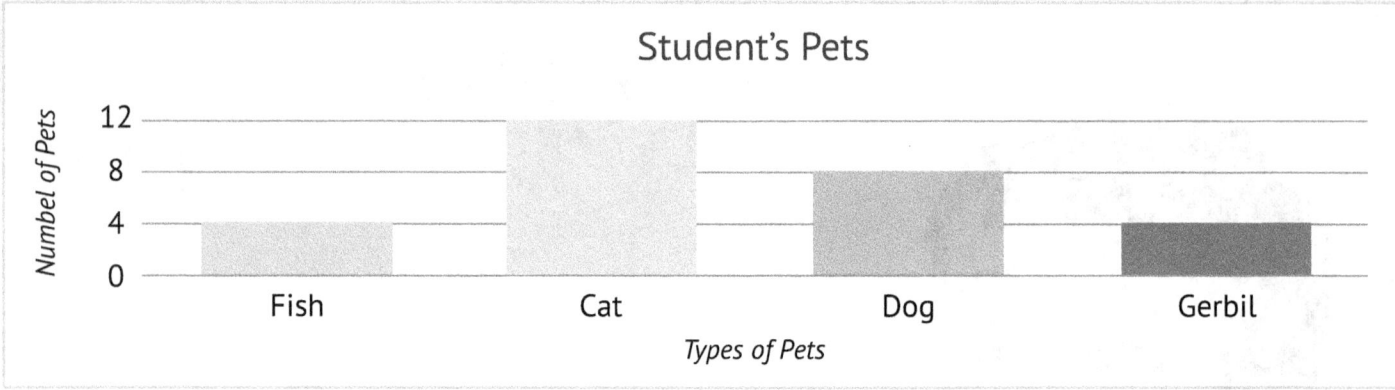

1. How many different types of pets are represented by this bar graph?

   A. 1
   B. 2
   C. 3
   D. 4

   3.MD.3

2. Which type of pet is *most* represented in this classroom?

   A. fish
   B. cat
   C. dog
   D. gerbil

   3.MD.3

3. How many students have a fish or a dog?

   A. 4
   B. 8
   C. 12
   D. 16

   3.MD.3

4. How many pets are there in the classroom altogether?

   A. 32   B. 30   C. 28   D. 26

   3.MD.3

5. What would be another good title for this bar graph?

   A. Pets in the Wild
   B. Our Classroom Pets
   C. How Many Pets
   D. Pet Store Animals

   3.MD.3

6. Which two pets were represented *equally* in this bar graph?

   A. fish and cats
   B. cats and gerbils
   C. fish and dogs
   D. fish and gerbils

   3.MD.3

When looking at a bar graph, pay attention to the values that the graph indicates. This will help you to figure out the values that the bars represent.

WEEK 14 : DAY 2

Use the following pictograph to answer questions 1-6.

Favorite Shapes in our classroom

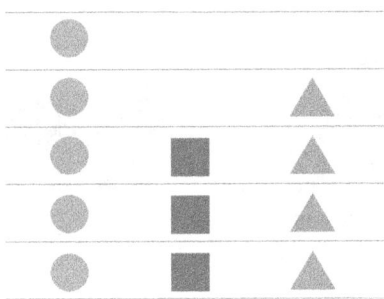

Circle   Square   Triangle

Key: Each shape is equal to 2 votes.

1. What type of data was collected to create this pictograph?
   A. Number of students in the classroom
   B. Number of shapes in the classroom
   C. Which shapes are the favorite in the classroom
   D. Which students are the favorite in the classroom

   3.MD.3

2. Which shape is the most popular in the classroom?
   A. Circle   C. Triangle
   B. Square   D. They are all equal

   3.MD.3

3. Based on the key, how many total students were asked what their favorite shape is?
   A. 12   C. 24
   B. 18   D. 26

   3.MD.3

4. How many more students liked circles than squares?
   A. 2 students   C. 5 students
   B. 4 students   D. 3 students

   3.MD.3

5. How many students liked squares or triangles best?
   A. 7 students
   B. 8 students
   C. 14 students
   D. 16 students

   3.MD.3

6. What would be another good title for this pictograph?
   A. Types of Shapes
   B. Colors of Shapes
   C. Shapes We Like
   D. Counting Shapes

   3.MD.3

TIP of the DAY

Pictographs often use pictures to represent values. Remember to consider how many items each picture represents. Sometimes one picture can represent more than one item.

WEEK 14 : DAY 3

Use the following bar graph to answer questions 1-5.

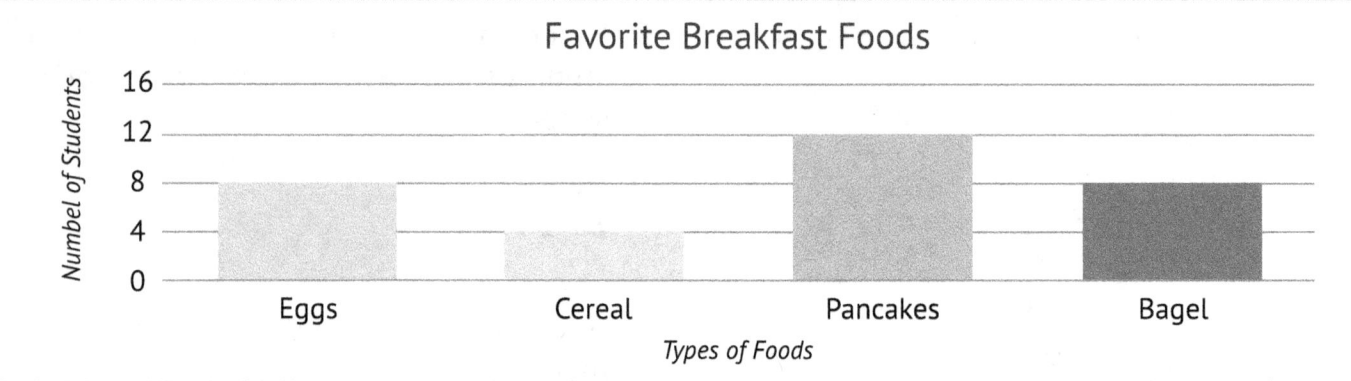

1. How many total students were asked what their favorite breakfast food is?

   A. 8
   B. 12
   C. 24
   D. 32

   3.MD.3

2. How many more students chose pancakes over cereal?

   A. 12
   B. 4
   C. 8
   D. 6

   3.MD.3

3. Hannah chose the **least** popular breakfast food. What is her favorite breakfast food?

   A. Eggs
   B. Cereal
   C. Pancakes
   D. Bagel

   3.MD.3

4. How many students chose eggs or pancakes?

   A. 20
   B. 18
   C. 16
   D. 12

   3.MD.3

5. Which of the following choices would be the best category to add to this graph?

   A. Steak
   B. Ice Cream
   C. Peach
   D. Waffle

   3.MD.3

TIP of the DAY

Graphs are a great way to understand a set or a group of data. Once you collect your data, turning it into a bar graph helps you to understand the information you collected.

WEEK 14 : DAY 4

Use the following bar graph to answer questions 1-5.

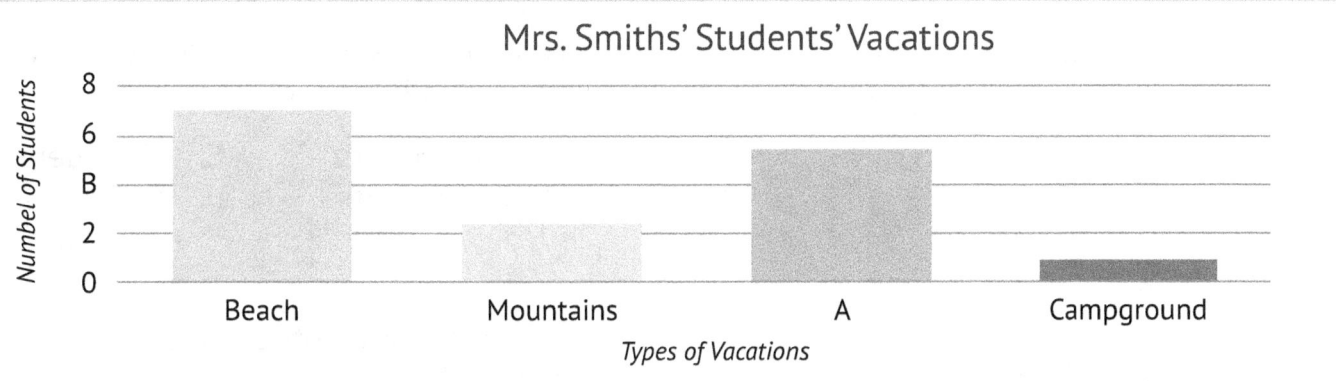

1. Jose chose the most popular vacation. Which vacation did Jose choose?

   A. Beach
   B. Mountains
   C. Vacation "A"
   D. Campground

   3.MD.3

2. What would be the *best* choice to fill in missing category "A"?

   A. Mall
   B. Movies
   C. Lake
   D. School

   3.MD.3

3. How many students chose the beach as their favorite vacation?

   A. 6
   B. 7
   C. 8
   D. 9

   3.MD.3

4. Which value best fills in the missing "B" for number of students?

   A. 2
   B. 3
   C. 4
   D. 5

   3.MD.3

5. Put the vacation choices in order from most popular to least popular.

   A. Beach, Mountains, Lake, Campground
   B. Campground, Lake, Mountains, Beach
   C. Beach, Lake, Campground, Mountains
   D. Beach, Lake, Mountains, Campground

   3.MD.3

When creating a bar graph, make sure to label everything! It's important to know what the graph is mostly about, and what the bars represent.

WEEK 14 : DAY 5

ASSESSMENT

Use the following pictograph to answer questions 1-4.

Classroom Favorite Stickers

Star   Smiley   Heart

Key: Each sticker represents 3 votes.

3. How many students were asked what their favorite sticker was?

   A. 30 students   C. 18 students
   B. 20 students   D. 9 students

   3.MD.3 / 3.OA.7

4. How many students chose star or smiley stickers?

   A. 9   C. 15
   B. 12   D. 18

   3.MD.3

1. Based on the key, how many students chose star stickers as their favorite?

   A. 3
   B. 4
   C. 6
   D. 9

   3.MD.3

5. Jermaine spent 64 cents on gum. If each piece cost 8 cents, how many pieces did he buy?

   A. 5 pieces   C. 7 pieces
   B. 6 pieces   D. 8 pieces

   3.OA.6 / 3.OA.7

2. Based on the key, how many more students chose heart stickers than smiley stickers?

   A. 2   C. 3
   B. 4   D. 8

   3.MD.3

6. What time is represented by a quarter till 9 at night?

   A. 9:15pm
   B. 8:45pm
   C. 9:15am
   D. 8:45am

   3.MD.1

DAY 6
Challenge question

Sharon arrived at the beach at 7:30pm. If it took her 3 hours and 25 minutes to get there, what time did she leave for the beach?

3.MD.3

96

WEEK 15

Fractions are back in Week 15! You will be measuring length using fractional units on an inch ruler. Measurements will include whole, half, and quarter inches. As well, you will be using line plots to understand data that has been collected in fractional units.

You can find detailed video explanations of each problem in the book by visiting: ArgoPrep.com

WEEK 15 : DAY 1

1. Based on the inch ruler, how long is the small box below?

   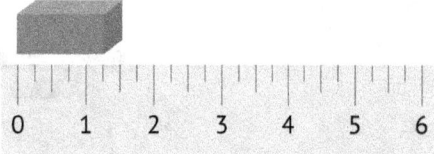

   A. 1 inch
   B. 2 inches
   C. 1 and $\frac{3}{4}$ inch
   D. 1 and $\frac{1}{4}$ inch

   3.MD.4

2. If an eraser is 2 inches long, how many half inches long is it?

   A. 2
   B. 3
   C. 4
   D. 5

   3.MD.4

3. Which of the following symbols makes the inequality **true**?

   1 and $\frac{1}{4}$ inch ☐ 1 and $\frac{1}{2}$ inch

   A. <
   B. >
   C. =
   D. +

   3.MD.4

4. Based on the inch ruler, how long is the post-it note below?

   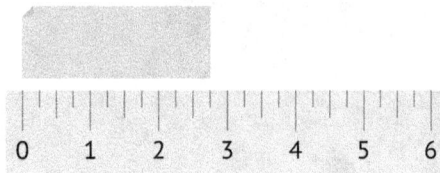

   A. 1 and $\frac{3}{4}$ inches
   B. 2 and $\frac{3}{4}$ inches
   C. 2 and $\frac{1}{2}$ inches
   D. 3 and $\frac{3}{4}$ inches

   3.MD.4

5. If a pencil is 5 and $\frac{3}{4}$ inches in length, which two whole inches would it fall between on a ruler?

   A. 3 and 4
   B. 4 and 5
   C. 5 and 6
   D. 6 and 7

   3.MD.4

TIP of the DAY

Just like fractions, inches can be divided equally into halves and fourths. Take a look at your ruler to see where each "half inch" and each "quarter inch" is marked.

WEEK 15 : DAY 2

1. Which of the following measurements could make the inequality *true*?

   3 and $\frac{1}{2}$ inches < [ ]

   A. 2 and $\frac{3}{4}$ in
   B. 3 in
   C. 3 and $\frac{1}{4}$ in
   D. 3 and $\frac{3}{4}$ in

   3.MD.4

2. Which measurement could fall between 4 and 5 inches on the ruler?

   A. 3 and $\frac{3}{4}$ in
   B. 4 and $\frac{3}{4}$ in
   C. 5 and $\frac{1}{4}$ in
   D. 5 and $\frac{3}{4}$ in

   3.MD.4

3. Based on the inch ruler, how long is the pink ribbon below?

   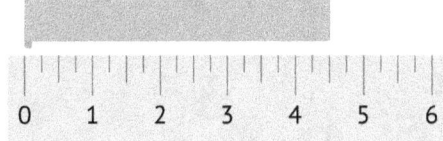

   A. 4 inches
   B. 4 and $\frac{1}{4}$ in
   C. 4 and $\frac{1}{2}$ in
   D. 4 and $\frac{3}{4}$ in

   3.MD.4

4. Yasmin has 2 pieces of string that are each 2 and $\frac{1}{4}$ inches long. How long is her string altogether?

   A. 4 and $\frac{2}{4}$ inches
   B. 4 and $\frac{1}{4}$ inches
   C. 3 and $\frac{1}{8}$ inches
   D. 3 and $\frac{2}{4}$ inches

   3.MD.4

5. Based on the inch ruler, how long is the strand of beads below?

   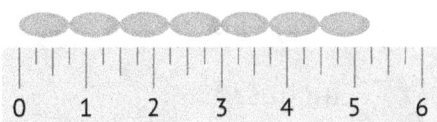

   A. 4 and $\frac{1}{4}$ inches
   B. 5 inches
   C. 5 and $\frac{1}{4}$ inches
   D. 5 and $\frac{1}{2}$ inches

   3.MD.4

TIP of the DAY

When measuring length, a "quarter inch" is one-fourth of an inch. A whole inch is made up of four "quarter inches."

WEEK 15 : DAY 3

Use the following line plot to answer questions 1-5.

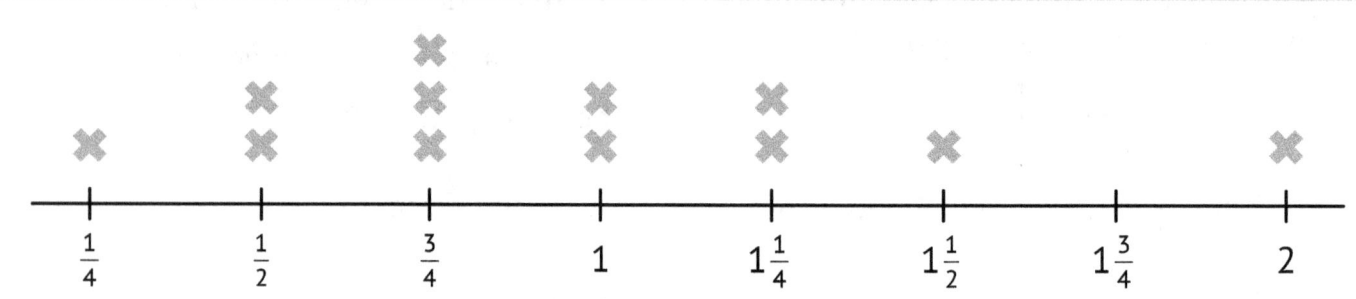

Rainy Days in August (in Inches)

1. If each x is equal to one day, how many days did it rain 1 and $\frac{1}{4}$ inches?

   A. 2   B. 3   C. 4   D. 5

   3.MD.4

2. How many days did it rain **less than or equal to** $\frac{3}{4}$ inches?

   A. 3   B. 4   C. 5   D. 6

   3.MD.4

3. How many days did it rain **more than** 1 and $\frac{1}{4}$ inches?

   A. 1   B. 2   C. 3   D. 4

   3.MD.4

4. Which amount of rain occurred the most in August?

   A. $\frac{1}{2}$ inch of rain

   B. $\frac{3}{4}$ inch of rain

   C. 1 and $\frac{1}{4}$ inches of rain

   D. 2 inches of rain

   3.MD.4

5. How many days did it rain in August?

   A. 12 days   C. 10 days
   B. 11 days   D. 9 days

   3.MD.4

TIP of the DAY

Line Plots represent data just like bar graphs and pictographs. Often times, they can represent data that is collected as fractions, like 1 and $\frac{1}{2}$ inches or 2 and $\frac{3}{4}$ inches.

100

WEEK 15 : DAY 4

Use the following line plot to answer questions 1-5.

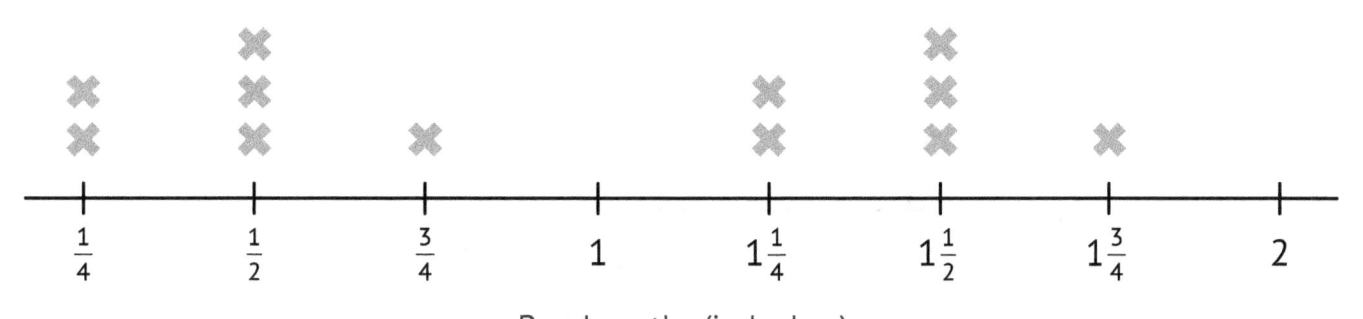

Bug Lengths (in Inches)

1. How many bugs were measured in all?

   A. 11 bugs
   B. 12 bugs
   C. 13 bugs
   D. 14 bugs

   3.MD.4

2. Which bug length was the **least** represented?

   A. $\frac{3}{4}$ in
   B. 1 in
   C. 1 and $\frac{1}{4}$ in
   D. 1 and $\frac{1}{2}$ in

   3.MD.4

3. How many bugs were 1 inch or **longer**?

   A. 9 bugs
   B. 8 bugs
   C. 7 bugs
   D. 6 bugs

   3.MD.4

4. How many bugs were $\frac{1}{4}$ inch or $\frac{1}{2}$ inch?

   A. 4 bugs
   B. 5 bugs
   C. 6 bugs
   D. 7 bugs

   3.MD.4

5. Which of the following statements is **true**?

   A. More bugs measured at less than one inch than more than one inch.
   B. More bugs measured at more than once inch than less than one inch.
   C. An equal amount of bugs were less than one inch and more than one inch.
   D. An unequal amount of bugs were less than one inch and more than. one inch

   3.MD.4

When using a ruler, make sure to note where the "whole" inches are. This will help you to estimate about how long your object is.

101

WEEK 15 : DAY 5

ASSESSMENT

Use the following line plot to answer questions 1-3.

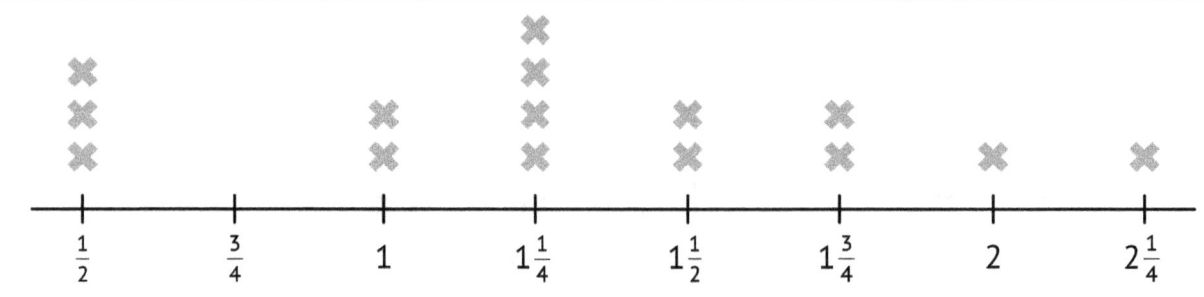

Length of Tomatoes Grown (in Inches)

1. Which length was the most common of the tomatoes that were grown?

   A. $\frac{1}{2}$ inch

   B. 1 inch

   C. 1 and $\frac{1}{4}$ inch

   D. 1 and $\frac{1}{2}$ inch

   3.MD.4

2. How many tomatoes were 1 and $\frac{1}{2}$ inches or **greater**?

   A. 5 tomatoes
   B. 6 tomatoes
   C. 7 tomatoes
   D. 8 tomatoes

   3.MD.4

3. How many tomatoes were grown in all?

   A. 13 tomatoes
   B. 14 tomatoes
   C. 15 tomatoes
   D. 16 tomatoes

   3.MD.4

4. Based on the inch ruler below, how long is the stick below?

   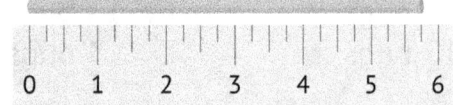

   A. 5 and $\frac{1}{4}$ in

   B. 5 and $\frac{1}{2}$ in

   C. 5 and $\frac{3}{4}$ in

   D. 6 and $\frac{3}{4}$ in

   3.MD.4

5. Mr. Hayes has 134 rocks in each of three buckets. **About** how many total rocks does he have in all three buckets, rounded to the nearest 10?

   A. 402
   B. 400
   C. 300
   D. 390

   3.NBT.1 / 3.NBT.2

DAY 6 Challenge question

Name three measurements that could come between 4 and 5 whole inches on a ruler?

3.MD.4

WEEK 16

VIDEO EXPLANATIONS ArgoPrep.com

Area is introduced in Week 16. Area is useful in finding out how much space a 2-dimensional object takes up. You will be asked to use drawings, models, arrays, and the standard algorithm to determine the area of different shapes.

You can find detailed video explanations of each problem in the book by visiting: ArgoPrep.com

WEEK 16 : DAY 1

1. What is the area of the rectangle below?

   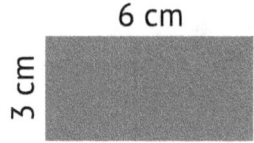

   A. 16 square cm C. 18 square cm
   B. 13 square cm D. 21 square cm

   3.MD.5

2. Mr. Bradley's garden is 5 feet by 8 feet. Which equation represents the area of his garden?

   A. 5 feet + 5 feet + 8 feet + 8 feet = = 26 square feet
   B. (5 feet x 5 feet) + (8 feet x 8 feet) = = 89 square feet
   C. 5 feet x 8 feet = 45 square feet
   D. 5 feet x 8 feet = 40 square feet

   3.MD.5

3. The farmer's plot of corn is 63 square feet. Based on the picture below, what is the length of his plot of corn?

   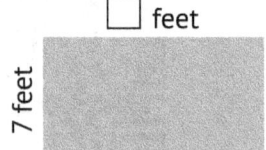

   A. 7 feet
   B. 8 feet
   C. 9 feet
   D. 10 feet

   3.MD.5 / 3.OA.6

4. Which of the following situations represents 2 inches × 9 inches = 18 square inches?

   A. Piece of paper that is 2 inches long and 9 inches wide
   B. Piece of paper that is 9 inches long and 9 inches wide
   C. 2 pieces of paper each 9 inches long and 9 inches wide
   D. 9 pieces of paper each 2 inches long and 2 inches wide

   3.MD.5

5. What is the area of a square that has a width of 7 cm?

   A. 7 square cm   C. 35 square cm
   B. 14 square cm D. 49 square cm

   3.MD.5

6. Kara is making a sandbox that is 4 feet wide. The length will be twice as long as the width. What will be the total area of her sandbox?

   A. 16 square feet
   B. 24 square feet
   C. 32 square feet
   D. 40 square feet

   3.MD.5

Area is the size of a surface, or how much space a 2-dimensional shape takes up. It's useful to know the area of a shape, so you can compare it to other shapes or surfaces.

WEEK 16 : DAY 2

1. The array below represents how big Geoffrey's painting is. What is the area of his painting?

   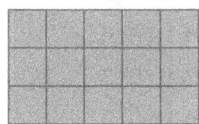

   A. 8 square units
   B. 15 square units
   C. 18 square units
   D. 20 square units

   3.MD.6

2. What is the area of a rectangle that is 7 inches long and 4 inches wide?

   A. 11 square inches
   B. 17 square inches
   C. 21 square inches
   D. 28 square inches

   3.MD.6

3. Which equation **would not** represent the following array?

   A. 2 inches x 7 inches = 14 square inches
   B. 2 inches ÷ 7 inches = 14 square inches
   C. 14 inches ÷ 7 inches = 2 square inches
   D. 14 inches ÷ 2 inches = 7 square inches

   3.MD.6

4. What would be the area of a square with a length of 9 units?

   A. 18 square units
   B. 27 square units
   C. 72 square units
   D. 81 square units

   3.MD.6

5. Catelyn is making a card for her grandmother. The paper she is using is 5 inches long and 7 inches wide. What is the area of the card?

   A. 35 square inches
   B. 30 square inches
   C. 25 square inches
   D. 20 square inches

   3.MD.6

6. What is the area of a rectangle that is 7 units wide and 8 units long?

   A. 48 square units
   B. 56 square units
   C. 64 square units
   D. 72 square units

   3.MD.6

TIP of the DAY

You can find the area of a shape by counting the amount of equal square units that it takes to fill in the shape. Square units are a tool for measuring area.

105

WEEK 16 : DAY 3

1. Krista has two pieces of paper that are both squares. If they have a length of 3 inches each, what is the total area of both pieces of paper?

   A. 9 square inches
   B. 18 square inches
   C. 27 square inches
   D. 36 square inches

   3.MD.5 / 3.OA.8

2. What is the area of the rectangular array shown below?

   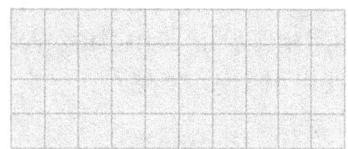

   A. 30 square units
   B. 36 square units
   C. 40 square units
   D. 44 square units

   3.MD.5 / 3.MD.6

3. Mr. Rogers has a garden with square feet sections. His garden has 4 rows of square feet and 9 columns of square feet. What is the total area of his garden?

   A. 32 square feet
   B. 36 square feet
   C. 40 square feet
   D. 44 square feet

   3.MD.5 / 3.MD.6

4. What is the area of a rectangle that is 3 units long and 12 units wide?

   A. 24 square units
   B. 36 square units
   C. 48 square units
   D. 60 square units

   3.MD.5 / 3.MD.6

5. Clarissa has a 45 square feet piece of fabric. If the width is 9 feet, what is the length?

   A. 5 feet   C. 7 feet
   B. 6 feet   D. 8 feet

   3.MD.5 / 3.OA.6

6. Carly makes a cake that is 4 cm by 11 cm. What is the area of her cake?

   A. 36 square cm   C. 44 square cm
   B. 40 square cm   D. 48 square cm

   3.MD.5 / 3.MD.6

7. Given the square units below, what is the area of the **whole** rectangle below?

   A. 7 square units
   B. 8 square units
   C. 12 square units
   D. 15 square units

   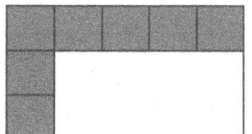

   3.MD.5 / 3.MD.6

TIP of the DAY

Arrays can help you find the area of a shape, like a square or a rectangle. Just count how many square units are in the shape, and you will find the area of the shape.

106

WEEK 16 : DAY 4

1. What is the width of a square that has an area of 25 square units?

    A. 25 square units
    B. 15 square units
    C. 10 square units
    D. 5 square units

    3.MD.5 / 3.OA.6

2. What is the area of the array below?

    A. 12 square units
    B. 15 square units
    C. 24 square units
    D. 27 square units

    3.MD.5 / 3.MD.6

3. What is the length of a square that has an area of 16 square cm?

    A. 4 cm
    B. 5 cm
    C. 6 cm
    D. 7 cm

    3.MD.5 / 3.MD.6

4. If the area of Mrs. Junska's coffee table is 15 square feet, how long is her table?

    A. 4 feet
    B. 5 feet
    C. 6 feet
    D. 7 feet

    3.MD.5 / 3.OA.6

5. What is the area of a rectangle that is 11 cm by 8 cm?

    A. 80 square cm
    B. 88 square cm
    C. 92 square cm
    D. 96 square cm

    3.MD.5 / 3.MD.6

6. Mr. Jaxon has a workbench made of wood boards that are each 1 square foot. The bench is 5 boards wide and 9 boards long. What is the area of his workbench?

    A. 35 square feet
    B. 40 square feet
    C. 45 square feet
    D. 50 square feet

    3.MD.5 / 3.MD.6

TIP of the DAY

The area of a shape can also be found by using multiplication. For example, if a rectangle is 4 square units wide and 5 square units long, multiply 4 x 5 for an area of 20 square units.

107

WEEK 16 : DAY 5

ASSESSMENT

1. The classroom rug is 7 feet by 12 feet. What is the area of the rug?

   A. 77 square feet
   B. 84 square feet
   C. 96 square feet
   D. 108 square feet

   3.MD.5

2. Given the square units below, what is the area of the **whole** rectangle below?

   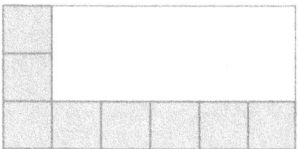

   A. 9 square units
   B. 12 square units
   C. 18 square units
   D. 21 square units

   3.MD.6

3. Jamie has two posters. They are both squares and both have a width of 4 feet. What is the total area of the posters?

   A. 16 square feet
   B. 24 square feet
   C. 28 square feet
   D. 32 square feet

   3.MD.5 / 3.OA.8

4. Janine went to the movies at 3:45pm. The movie she saw lasted 1 hour and 20 minutes. What time did she leave the movies?

   A. 4:05pm   C. 5:05pm
   B. 4:45pm   D. 5:45pm

   3.MD.1

5. Which of the following fractions is the *largest*?

   A. $\frac{2}{6}$ C. $\frac{2}{4}$
   B. $\frac{2}{5}$ D. $\frac{2}{3}$

   3.NF.3

6. If the total area of the picnic table is 42 feet squared, what is the length?

   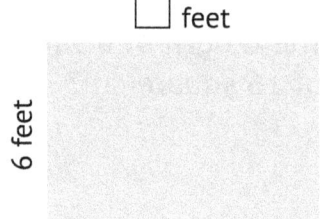

   A. 6 feet   C. 8 feet
   B. 7 feet   D. 9 feet

   3.MD.5 / 3.OA.6

DAY 6 Challenge question

Callie has a sandbox that is 4 feet by 5 feet. Hannah has a sandbox that has an area twice as big as Callie's. What is the area of Hannah's sandbox?

3.MD.5

WEEK 17

ARGOPREP.COM

VIDEO
EXPLANATIONS

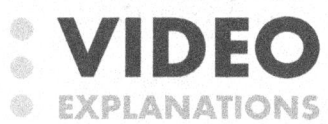

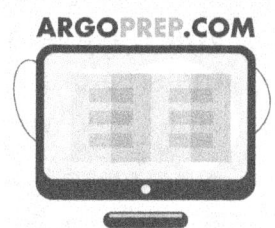

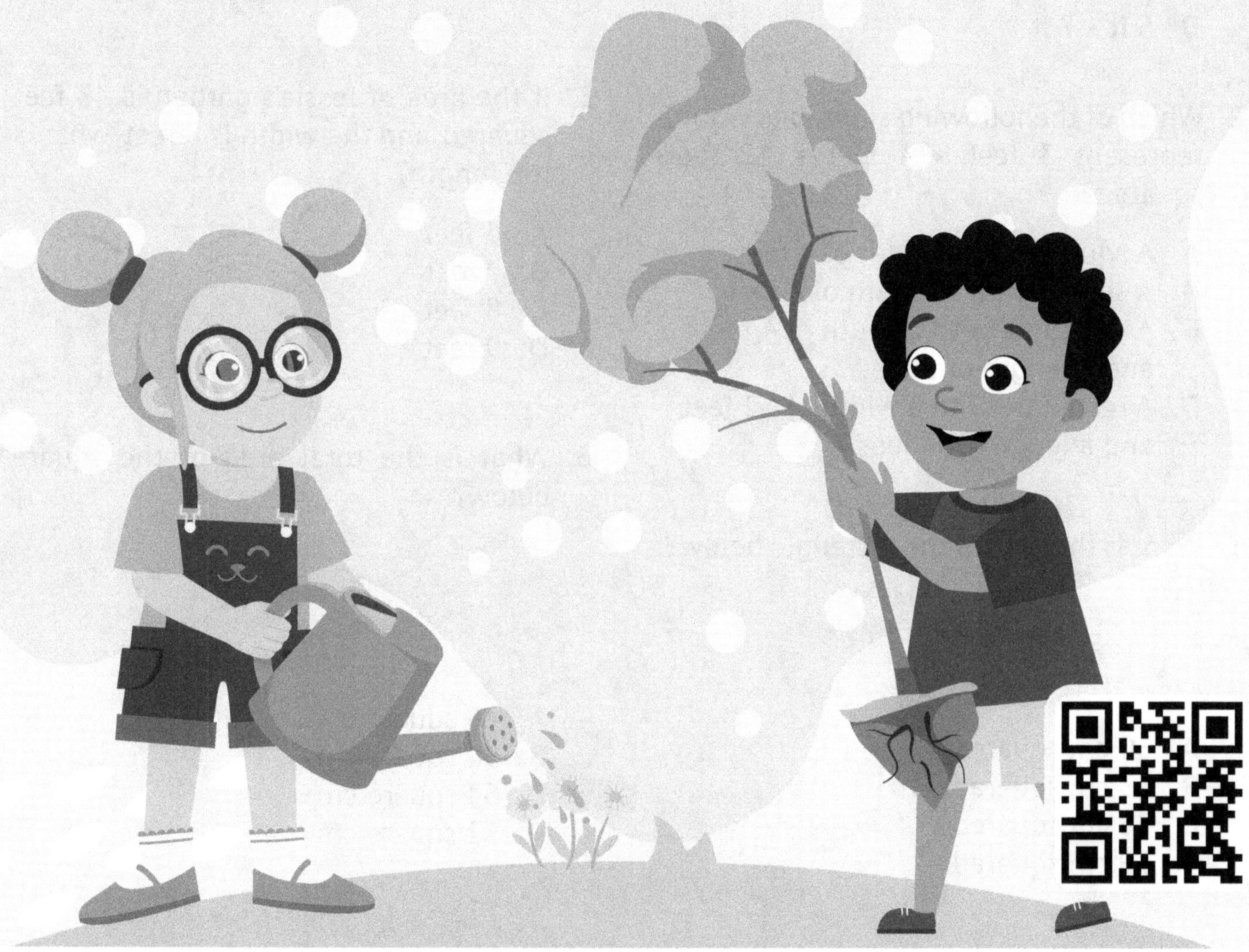

Week 17 will give you even more practice with area in real-world situations. You will be asked to use your understanding of area, multiplication and division to find unknown factors in an equation or situation. What better way to review those multiplication facts!

You can find detailed video explanations of each problem in the book by visiting: ArgoPrep.com

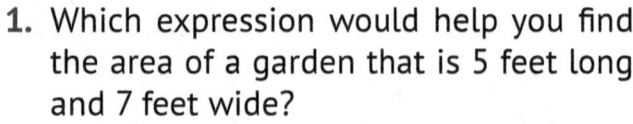

WEEK 17 : DAY 1

1. Which expression would help you find the area of a garden that is 5 feet long and 7 feet wide?

   A. 5 ft + 5 ft + 7 ft + 7 ft
   B. (5 ft + 5 ft) x (7 ft + 7 ft)
   C. (5 ft x 7 ft) + (5 ft x 7 ft)
   D. 5 ft x 7 ft

   3.MD.7

2. Which of the following situations would represent 3 feet x 4 feet = 12 feet squared?

   A. A square with a width of 4 feet
   B. A square with a length of 4 feet
   C. A rectangle with a width of 4 feet and a length of 3 feet
   D. A rectangle with a width of 12 feet and a length of 3 feet

   3.MD.7

3. What is the area of the rectangle below?

   11 cm
   3 cm

   A. 30 cm squared
   B. 33 cm squared
   C. 36 cm squared
   D. 39 cm squared

   3.MD.7

4. If the side table is 12 inches by 12 inches, what is the total area?

   A. 124 inches squared
   B. 136 inches squared
   C. 144 inches squared
   D. 156 inches squared

   3.MD.7

5. If the area of Jessie's garden is 48 feet squared, and the width is 8 feet, what is the length?

   A. 6 feet
   B. 7 feet
   C. 8 feet
   D. 9 feet

   3.MD.7

6. What is the total area of the square below?

   8 cm

   A. 48 square cm
   B. 56 square cm
   C. 64 square cm
   D. 72 square cm

   3.MD.7

TIP of the DAY

Multiplication is an easy way to find the area of a shape, like a square or rectangle. Multiply the width and the length together and you will find the total area.

110

WEEK 17 : DAY 2

1. The rectangle below represents one section of Michele's garden. If she has 4 equal sections in her garden, what is the total area of her garden?

   A. 8 square feet
   B. 16 square feet
   C. 24 square feet
   D. 32 square feet

   3.MD.7

2. The classroom is divided into two sections. Each section is 8 feet wide by 12 feet long. What is the total area of the whole classroom?

   A. 96 feet^2
   B. 190 feet^2
   C. 192 feet^2
   D. 288 feet^2

   3.MD.7 / 3.NBT.2

3. Janie has three pieces of carpet. What is the total area of the 3 pieces of carpet?

   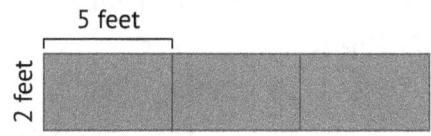

   A. 10 square feet
   B. 20 square feet
   C. 30 square feet
   D. 40 square feet

   3.MD.7

4. Joni's poster board is 4 feet by 3 feet. If she wants to cut her poster board in half, what would be the total area?

   A. 12 square feet
   B. 10 square feet
   C. 8 square feet
   D. 6 square feet

   3.MD.7

5. The whole playground is 10 feet by 11 feet. There is a patch of grass that is 7 feet by 4 feet. What is the area of the playground that is *not* grass?

   A. 110 square feet
   B. 82 square feet
   C. 28 square feet
   D. 111 square feet

   3.MD.7 / 3.OA.8

6. What is the area of a picture frame that is 12 inches by 4 inches?

   A. 24 square inches
   B. 36 square inches
   C. 48 square inches
   D. 56 square inches

   3.MD.7

TIP of the DAY

Area can be found for any square unit: square centimeters, square inches, square feet, or square miles. Think about how big a square mile might be!

WEEK 17 : DAY 3

1. Using square units, what is the area of the shape below?

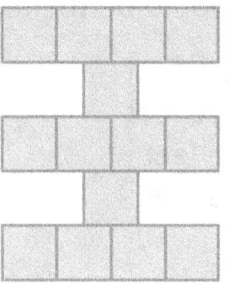

   A. 12 square units
   B. 14 square units
   C. 16 square units
   D. 18 square units

3.MD.7

2. What is the area of a square that has a width of 9 feet?

   A. 72 square feet
   B. 79 square feet
   C. 81 square feet
   D. 99 square feet

3.MD.7

3. The shaded areas represent sections of the park that are grass. What is the total area of grass in the park?

   A. 5 square units
   B. 10 square units
   C. 15 square units
   D. 20 square units

3.MD.7

4. What are the side lengths of a square that has an area of 49 units squared?

   A. 5 units   C. 7 units
   B. 6 units   D. 8 units

3.MD.7

5. Janie has pieces of tape below. Each piece is 2 cm by 4 cm. What is the total area of tape?

   A. 40 square cm
   B. 38 square cm
   C. 32 square cm
   D. 28 square cm

3.MD.7 / 3.OA.8

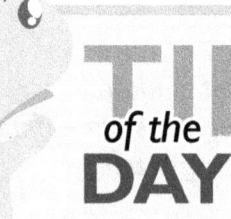

TIP of the DAY

To find the area of an oddly shaped figure, like a kitchen counter, find the area of two rectangles that make up the entire figure and then add their individual areas together to find the total area.

WEEK 17 : DAY 4

1. What is the area of the shape below?

   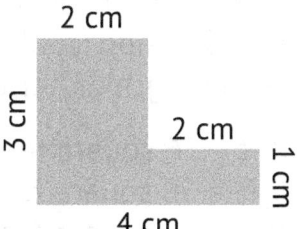

   A. 8 square cm   C. 36 square cm
   B. 12 square cm   D. 48 square cm

   3.MD.7

2. Mrs. Winslow has a garden that has an area of 60 square feet. Which of the following equations could represent the width and length of her garden?

   A. 6 ft × 12 ft = 60 square feet
   B. 5 ft × 10 ft = 60 square feet
   C. 6 ft × 10 ft = 60 square feet
   D. 5 ft × 11 ft = 60 square feet

   3.MD.7

3. Deanna's kitchen has 10 square tiles. Each tile has a width of 2 feet. What is the total area of her kitchen tiles?

   A. 20 square feet
   B. 40 square feet
   C. 80 square feet
   D. 200 square feet

   3.MD.7 / 3.OA.8

4. What is the area of the shape below?

   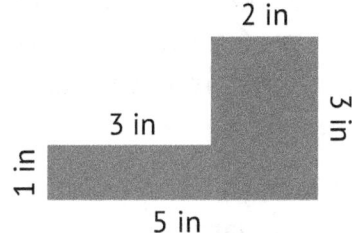

   A. 30 square in   C. 14 square in
   B. 21 square in   D. 9 square in

   3.MD.7

5. Julio has a rug that is 6 feet by 7 feet. There is a blue square in the middle that has an area of 18 square feet. What is the area of the rug that is not covered by the blue square?

   A. 18 square feet
   B. 24 square feet
   C. 42 square feet
   D. 60 square feet

   3.MD.7

6. What is the length of a rectangle that has a total area of 56 inches and a width of 7 inches?

   A. 8 inches   C. 10 inches
   B. 9 inches   D. 11 inches

   3.MD.7 / 3.OA.6

Since squares always have the same width and length, you only need to know the length of one side. Just multiply one side length by itself and you will find the total area.

113

WEEK 17 : DAY 5

ASSESSMENT

1. The park has a length of 9 yards by 8 yards. The basketball court has a length of 5 yards by 6 yards. What is the area of the park that is *not* taken up by the basketball court?

   A. 72 square yards
   B. 30 square yards
   C. 102 square yards
   D. 42 square yards

   3.MD.7

2. Yessamyn has papers that she wants to tape together to make a sign. Each paper is 3 inches by 5 inches. What is the total area of her sign going to be?

   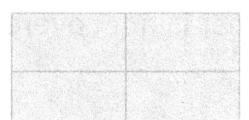

   A. 15 square inches
   B. 30 square inches
   C. 45 square inches
   D. 60 square inches

   3.MD.7

3. What is the order of the fractions, from *greatest to least*?

   $$\frac{1}{4}, \frac{1}{3}, \frac{1}{8}, \frac{1}{2}$$

   A. $\frac{1}{8}, \frac{1}{4}, \frac{1}{3}, \frac{1}{2}$
   C. $\frac{1}{2}, \frac{1}{3}, \frac{1}{4}, \frac{1}{8}$
   B. $\frac{1}{3}, \frac{1}{2}, \frac{1}{8}, \frac{1}{4}$
   D. $\frac{1}{4}, \frac{1}{3}, \frac{1}{8}, \frac{1}{2}$

   3.NF.3

4. Kelsey is getting new carpet for her bedroom. If the carpet covers 56 square feet, what expression could represent the width and length of her bedroom?

   A. 7 ft × 8 ft = 56 square feet
   B. 8 ft × 9 ft = 56 square feet
   C. 6 ft × 8 ft = 56 square feet
   D. 7 ft × 9 ft = 56 square feet

   3.OA.6

5. There are 234 basketballs and 371 tennis balls in the gym. *About* how many balls are there altogether in the gym, rounded to the nearest hundred?

   A. 605
   B. 600
   C. 610
   D. 620

   3.NBT.1 / 3.NBT.2

6. What is the area of the shape below?

   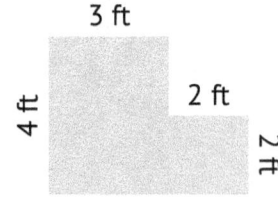

   A. 16 square feet
   B. 12 square feet
   C. 10 square feet
   D. 8 square feet

   3.MD.7

DAY 6
Challenge question

The classroom is 12 by 12 feet. The rectangle carpet covers an area that is 4 feet wide and 9 feet long. What area of the classroom floor is *not* covered by the carpet?

3.MD.7

WEEK 18

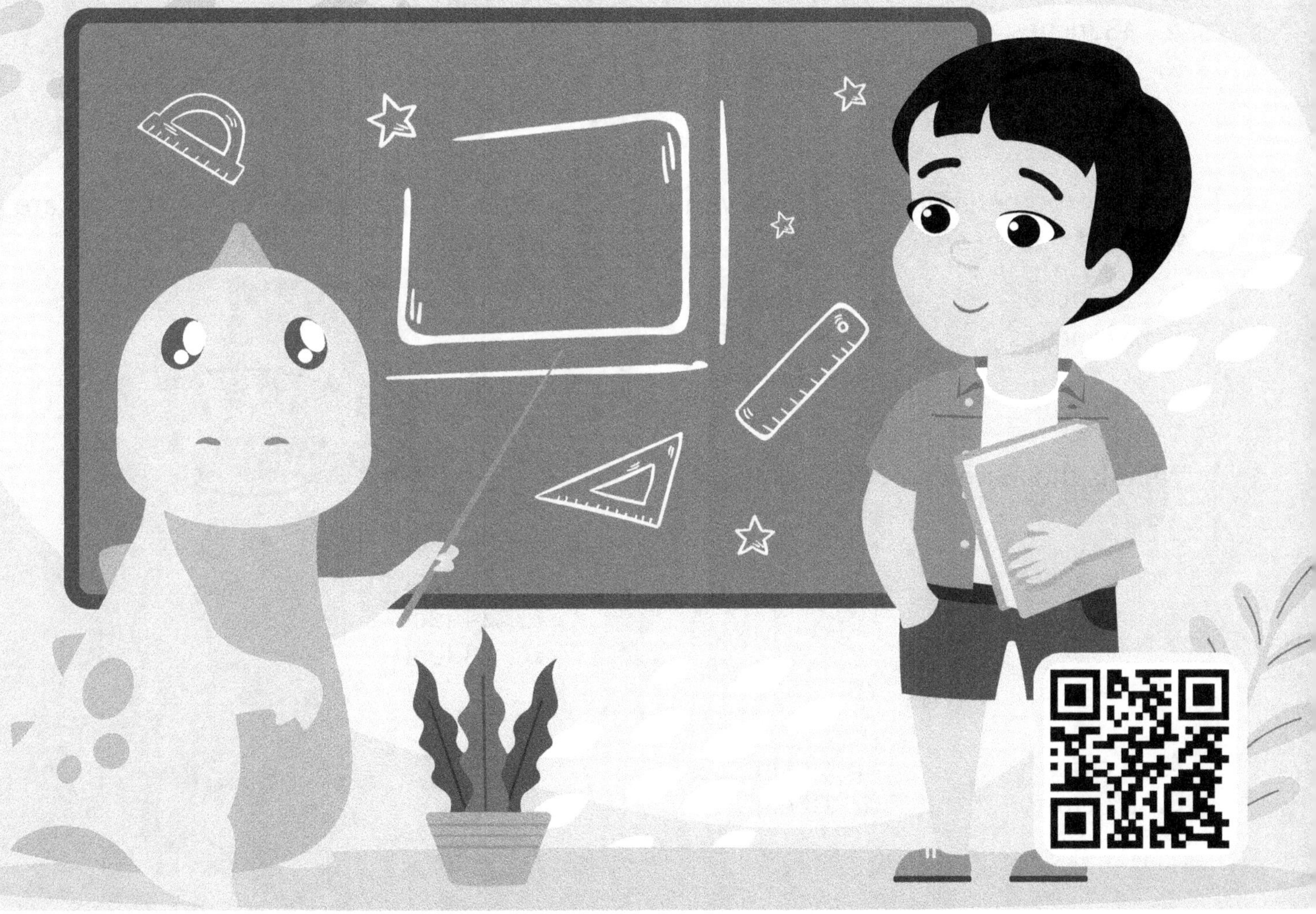

This week involves a close relative of area: perimeter. Week 18 will allow you to find the total perimeter given all sides, or to determine a missing side length when you know the total perimeter. Real-world situations will be included as always.

You can find detailed video explanations of each problem in the book by visiting: ArgoPrep.com

WEEK 18 : DAY 1

1. What is the perimeter of this rectangle?

   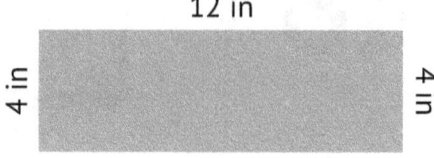

   A. 48 inches
   B. 36 inches
   C. 32 inches
   D. 24 inches

2. What is the perimeter of square with a width of 8 inches?

   A. 16 inches
   B. 32 inches
   C. 48 inches
   D. 64 inches

3. What is the perimeter of this polygon?

   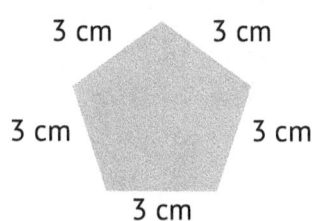

   A. 9 cm
   B. 12 cm
   C. 15 cm
   D. 18 cm

4. What is the perimeter of a rectangle with a width of 12 inches and a length of 9 inches?

   A. 42 inches
   B. 60 inches
   C. 72 inches
   D. 108 inches

5. What is the perimeter of the square below?

   A. 36 feet
   B. 30 feet
   C. 24 feet
   D. 18 feet

TIP of the DAY: The perimeter helps us to find the total distance around a polygon. If you know the lengths of all sides of a polygon, you can add them together to find the perimeter.

WEEK 18 : DAY 2

1. If a polygon has 6 equal sides, and each of those sides have a length of 7 inches, what is the perimeter of the polygon?

   A. 42 inches C. 28 inches
   B. 35 inches D. 21 inches

   3.MD.8

2. The total perimeter of the rectangle below is 24. What is the length of the missing side?

   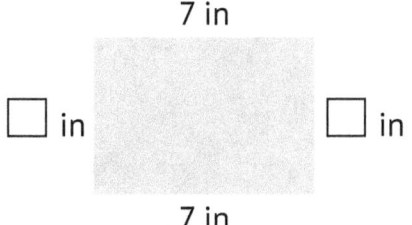

   A. 3 inches C. 5 inches
   B. 4 inches D. 6 inches

   3.MD.8

3. What is the perimeter of a square that has a length of 9 inches?

   A. 81 inches
   B. 72 inches
   C. 45 inches
   D. 36 inches

   3.MD.8

4. Sara Jane has a piece of paper that is 7 inches wide. If the length is twice as long as the width, what is the total perimeter of Sara Jane's paper?

   A. 14 inches C. 42 inches
   B. 28 inches D. 49 inches

   3.MD.8

5. What is the perimeter of the polygon below?

   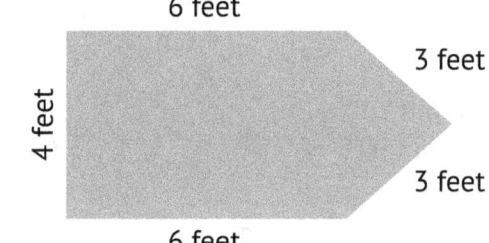

   A. 22 inches C. 14 inches
   B. 18 inches D. 12 inches

   3.MD.8

6. What is the perimeter of a rectangle with a width of 7 cm and a length of 4 cm?

   A. 28 cm
   B. 24 cm
   C. 22 cm
   D. 20 cm

   3.MD.8

The opposite sides of a rectangle will always be the same length. Therefore, if the length of one rectangle side is unknown, just look at the length of the opposite side.

WEEK 18 : DAY 3

1. Mrs. Jacob's garden is 8 feet in length. The width is *half* as much as the length. What is the perimeter of her garden?

   A. 32 feet C. 16 feet
   B. 24 feet D. 8 feet

   3.MD.8

2. If the perimeter of the polygon below is 20 cm, what is the length of the missing side?

   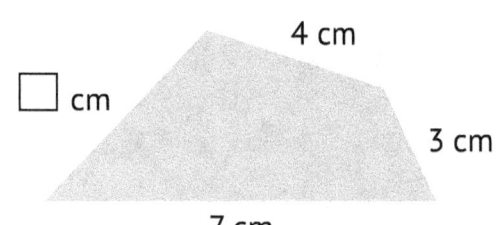

   A. 7 cm C. 5 cm
   B. 6 cm D. 4 cm

   3.MD.8

3. What is the perimeter of a polygon that has 5 equal sides that are all 8 inches long?

   A. 40 inches C. 56 inches
   B. 48 inches D. 64 inches

   3.MD.8

4. Jamill wants to make a table that has a perimeter of 14 feet. If the width of his table is 4 feet, what will be the length of his table?

   A. 18 feet C. 4 feet
   B. 14 feet D. 3 feet

   3.MD.8

5. What is the perimeter of the triangle below?

   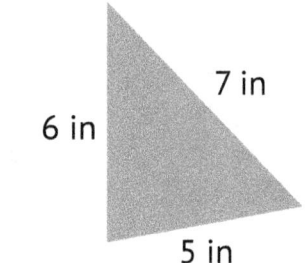

   A. 30 inches C. 18 inches
   B. 24 inches D. 12 inches

   3.MD.8

6. What is the perimeter of a square that has an area of 25 square feet?

   A. 20 feet C. 10 feet
   B. 15 feet D. 5 feet

   3.MD.8

TIP of the DAY

The four side lengths of a square will always be equal. Therefore, if you know one side length, you can add that amount together four times and find the perimeter.

WEEK 18 : DAY 4

1. If the rectangle below has an area of 16 square inches, what is the perimeter?

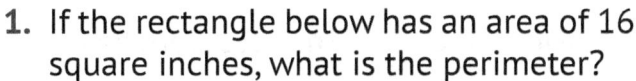

   A. 64 inches
   B. 32 inches
   C. 20 inches
   D. 16 inches

   3.MD.8

2. Julius has a square table that has an area of 64 square inches. What is the perimeter of his table?

   A. 8 inches
   B. 16 inches
   C. 24 inches
   D. 32 inches

   3.MD.7 / 3.MD.8

3. All the sides of the star below are equal. What is the perimeter of the star?

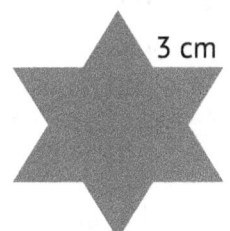

   A. 36 cm
   B. 33 cm
   C. 30 cm
   D. 27 cm

   3.MD.8

4. What is *true* about these two rectangles?

   A. They have the same perimeter, but different area.
   B. They have the same area, but different perimeter.
   C. They have the same area and the same perimeter.
   D. They have a different area and a different perimeter.

   3.MD.7 / 3.MD.8

5. The perimeter of a square is 12 inches. What is the **area**?

   A. 6 square inches
   B. 9 square inches
   C. 12 square inches
   D. 15 square inches

   3.MD.7 / 3.MD.8

TIP of the DAY

If you know the total perimeter of a polygon, but are missing one side length, just subtract all the other side lengths from the total perimeter. This will help you to find your missing side length.

WEEK 18 : DAY 5

ASSESSMENT

1. What is the perimeter of a polygon with 7 equal sides that all have lengths of 5 inches?

   A. 28 inches C. 42 inches
   B. 35 inches D. 49 inches

   3.MD.8

2. What is *true* about these two rectangles?

   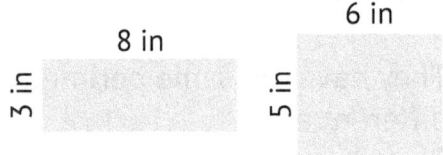

   A. They have the same perimeter, but different area.
   B. They have the same area, but different perimeter.
   C. They have the same area and the same perimeter.
   D. They have a different area and a different perimeter.

   3.MD.7 / 3.MD.8

3. Kamill has a square poster that has an area of 36 square inches. What is the perimeter of his poster?

   A. 20 inches C. 28 inches
   B. 24 inches D. 32 inches

   3.MD.7 / 3.MD.8

4. Jessie has run $\frac{2}{5}$ of the race, Sam has run $\frac{2}{6}$ of the race, Hank has run $\frac{2}{8}$ of the race, and Shaynell has run $\frac{2}{3}$ of the race. Who has run the **least** amount?

   A. Jessie   C. Hank
   B. Sam   D. Shaynell

   3.NF.3

5. The movie theater had 5 visitors on Monday, 10 on Tuesday, and 20 on Wednesday. If the pattern continues, how many visitors will there be on Friday?

   A. 40 visitors   C. 80 visitors
   B. 60 visitors   D. 100 visitors

   3.OA.9

6. The perimeter of the polygon below is 24. What is the length of the missing side?

   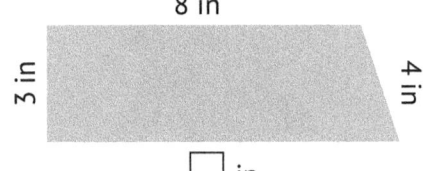

   A. 6 inches   C. 8 inches
   B. 7 inches   D. 9 inches

   3.MD.8

DAY 6
Challenge question

A rectangular poster has an area of 24 square inches. What are two different pairs of side lengths that this poster could have?

3.OA.7

120

WEEK 19

VIDEO EXPLANATIONS

ARGOPREP.COM

Week 19 is all about shapes. You will review concepts and characteristics of polygons that you already know. This week will also take a special look at quadrilaterals: squares, rectangles, trapezoids, and rhombuses.

**You can find detailed video explanations of each problem in the book by visiting:
ArgoPrep.com**

WEEK 19 : DAY 1

1. What of the following is **not true** about a square?

   A. The sides are all the same length
   B. The sides are all straight lines
   C. There are four square corners
   D. The sides are all different lengths

   3.G.1

2. What could the following shape **not** be called?

   A. Square
   B. Polygon
   C. Quadrilateral
   D. Trapezoid

   3.G.1

3. Why is the following shape **not** a polygon?

   A. Because it only has three sides
   B. Because it is not colored in
   C. Because it has only one angle
   D. Because it is not made of all straight lines

   3.G.1

4. Which statement is true about the two shapes below?

    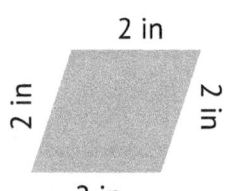

   A. They both have the same perimeter.
   B. They both have all unequal sides.
   C. They both have all equal sides.
   D. They are both squares.

   3.G.1

5. What is the name of the solid shape below?

   A. Cube
   B. Cylinder
   C. Rectangular Prism
   D. Pyramid

   3.G.1

TIP of the DAY

Rectangles and squares are both made with 4 straight lines. Rectangles have two sets of equal sides with equal lengths, while all sides of a square are equal in length.

122

WEEK 19 : DAY 2

1. What are two quadrilaterals that always have four right angles?

   A. Square and Rhombus
   B. Square and Trapezoid
   C. Rectangle and Square
   D. Rectangle and Trapezoid

   3.G.1

2. What is the name of the quadrilateral below?

   A. Square
   B. Trapezoid
   C. Rhombus
   D. Rectangle

   3.G.1

3. Which quadrilateral can have four equal sides, but no right angles?

   A. Square
   B. Trapezoid
   C. Rhombus
   D. Rectangle

   3.G.1

4. Marley has a table with four right corners, with two sets of sides that are equal, but not all sides equal. What is the shape of her table?

   A. Square
   B. Trapezoid
   C. Rhombus
   D. Rectangle

   3.G.1

5. Which two quadrilaterals have all equal sides?

   A. Square and Rhombus
   B. Square and Trapezoid
   C. Rectangle and Square
   D. Rectangle and Trapezoid

   3.G.1

6. Which of the following quadrilateral names could the shape below *not* be called?

   A. Square
   B. Trapezoid
   C. Rhombus
   D. Rectangle

   3.G.1

TIP of the DAY

Quadrilaterals are polygons with four sides. A quadrilateral could have all sides with equal lengths, like a square or rhombus, or no sides with equal lengths, like a trapezoid.

WEEK 19 : DAY 3

1. What is the name of the polygon below?

   A. Square
   B. Rectangle
   C. Parallelogram
   D. Rhombus

   3.G.1

2. Which statement is *true* about parallelograms?

   A. They have two sets of opposite parallel sides.
   B. They have one set of opposite parallel sides.
   C. They have four equal sides.
   D. They have four right angles.

   3.G.1

3. Hester has a parallelogram with all equal sides. What shape could he have?

   A. Triangle   C. Trapezoid
   B. Rectangle   D. Square

   3.G.1

4. How many sets of opposite parallel sides does a Trapezoid have?

   A. 0 sets   C. 2 sets
   B. 1 set   D. 3 sets

   3.G.1

5. What name would you not call the shape below?

   A. Rectangle
   B. Quadrilateral
   C. Rhombus
   D. Parallelogram

   3.G.1

TIP of the DAY

A parallelogram is a type of quadrilateral that has two sets of parallel sides. A rectangle, a square, and a rhombus are all parallelograms.

WEEK 19 : DAY 4

1. Camille has a shape that has four equal sides, two sets of parallel sides, but no right angles. What shape could she have?

   A. Square
   B. Trapezoid
   C. Rhombus
   D. Rectangle

   3.G.1

2. Which of the following are always considered parallelograms?

   A. square and rectangle only
   B. square and rhombus only
   C. trapezoid, rhombus and square
   D. rectangle, rhombus and square

   3.G.1

3. Which shapes are characterized by *always* having four equal sides and two sets of parallel lines?

   A. rhombus and trapezoid only
   B. rhombus and rectangle only
   C. square and rhombus only
   D. square and trapezoid only

   3.G.1

4. Luke thinks the shape below is a parallelogram. Is he correct?

   A. Yes, because there are four straight sides.
   B. Yes, because there is one set of parallel lines.
   C. No, because there are not four right angles.
   D. No, because there are not two sets of parallel lines.

   3.G.1

5. Mr. Harrison has a piece of paper that has side lengths of 4 cm, 5 cm, 6 cm, and 2 cm. What shape could he have?

   A. Square   C. Trapezoid
   B. Rhombus   D. Rectangle

   3.G.1

6. How many sets of parallel sides does a Rhombus have?

   A. 0 sets   C. 2 sets
   B. 1 set   D. 3 sets

   3.G.1

TIP of the DAY

A rhombus is like a square, in that all sides have equal lengths. A rhombus is different from a square in that it does not always have four right angles, or square corners.

125

WEEK 19 : DAY 5

ASSESSMENT

1. What name would you *not* use to describe the shape below?

   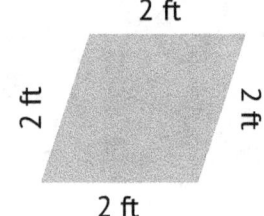

   A. Square
   B. Rhombus
   C. Quadrilateral
   D. Parallelogram

   3.G.1

2. Keil's garden has side lengths of 4 feet, 5 feet, 3 feet, and 6 feet. What could be the shape of his garden?

   A. Square
   B. Trapezoid
   C. Rhombus
   D. Rectangle

   3.G.1

3. The poster in the library is rhombus shaped. If one side length is 11 inches long, what is the perimeter of the poster?

   A. 22 inches
   B. 33 inches
   C. 44 inches
   D. 55 inches

   3.G.1 / 3.MD.8

4. The Third Grade is collecting recycled bottles. One class collected 234 bottles, one class collected 324 bottles, and one class collected 198 bottles. How many bottles have they collected all together?

   A. 558 bottles
   B. 756 bottles
   C. 757 bottles
   D. 766 bottles

   3.NBT.2

5. Darnell arrived at the beach at 3:45 in the afternoon. If it took him 4 hours and 30 minutes to drive to the beach, what time did he leave for the beach?

   A. 11:15 at night
   B. 11:15 in the morning
   C. 12:15 at night
   D. 12:15 in the morning

   3.MD.1

6. Justin's poster has four equal sides, two sets of parallel sides, but no right angles. What shape is his poster?

   A. Square
   B. Trapezoid
   C. Rectangle
   D. Rhombus

   3.G.1

DAY 6
Challenge question

Kylie has two shapes, a square and a rhombus. Both shapes have side lengths of 12 inches. What is the sum when you combine the perimeter of both shapes?

3.G.2 / 3.MD.8

126

WEEK 20

VIDEO EXPLANATIONS
ARGOPREP.COM

We will combine fractions and shapes in Week 20. Partitioning shapes into equal sections will be a big focus. You will also be given opportunities to name and identify shapes and situations that represent fractions and unit fractions.

You can find detailed video explanations of each problem in the book by visiting:
ArgoPrep.com

WEEK 20 : DAY 1

1. Which of the following is partitioned into 4 equal parts?

    A.
    B.
    C.
    D.

    3.G.2

2. Gerard has a cake that he cuts into 5 equal pieces. Which fraction represents two of those pieces?

    A. $\dfrac{1}{5}$ B. $\dfrac{2}{5}$ C. $\dfrac{5}{2}$ D. $\dfrac{5}{1}$

    3.G.2

3. If one of the equal pieces below was shaded in, which fraction would represent the shaded part?

    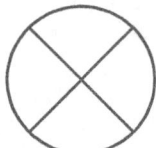

    A. $\dfrac{1}{4}$ B. $\dfrac{1}{3}$ C. $\dfrac{3}{4}$ D. $\dfrac{4}{1}$

    3.G.2

4. Which fraction represents the unshaded portion of the shape below?

    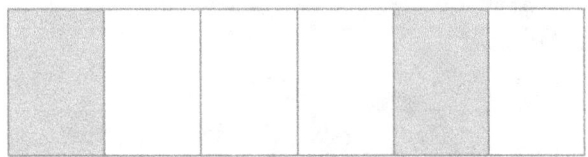

    A. $\dfrac{2}{4}$ C. $\dfrac{4}{6}$

    B. $\dfrac{2}{6}$ D. $\dfrac{1}{6}$

    3.G.2

5. Carol has a piece of paper that she divides into 8 equal sections. She colors on 5 of the sections. Which fraction represents the sections she **did not** color on?

    A. $\dfrac{3}{5}$ C. $\dfrac{3}{8}$

    B. $\dfrac{5}{3}$ D. $\dfrac{5}{8}$

    3.G.2

TIP of the DAY

A shape has to be divided into equal parts to be able to assign a unit fraction. If a shape has three parts, and they are equal in size, each of them would be called $\dfrac{1}{3}$.

WEEK 20 : DAY 2

1. Which of the following models shows $\frac{3}{4}$?

    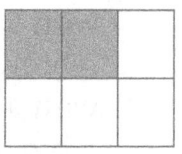
   Model A   Model B   Model C

   A. Model A only
   B. Model B only
   C. Model A and C
   D. Model B and C

2. Which situation best represents $\frac{2}{4}$?

   A. A cake cut into 2 equal pieces, and 4 have been eaten
   B. A cake cut into 2 equal pieces, and 2 have been eaten
   C. A cake cut into 4 equal pieces, and 2 have been eaten
   D. A cake cut into 4 equal pieces, and 4 have been eaten

3. What fraction of the shape below is shaded?

   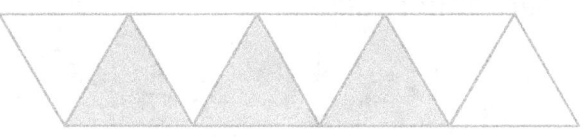

   A. $\frac{3}{5}$ B. $\frac{3}{8}$ C. $\frac{5}{8}$ D. $\frac{3}{6}$

4. Which fraction represents one piece of a brownie that has been divided into 3 equal pieces?

   A. $\frac{3}{3}$ B. $\frac{3}{1}$ C. $\frac{2}{3}$ D. $\frac{1}{3}$

5. Sarai has a rectangle that is divided into 8 equal parts, with 4 shaded in. Which shape below **would not** represent her rectangle?

   A.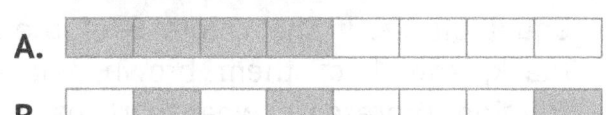
   B.
   C.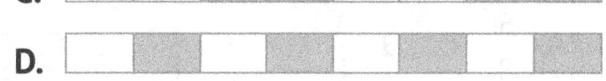
   D.

TIP of the DAY

The denominator helps you to know how many equal parts a shape is partitioned into. If your denominator is "5", you will have five equal parts.

WEEK 20 : DAY 3

1. Helena's cake was divided into 4 equal parts. What fraction could represent part of her cake?

   A. $\frac{4}{8}$ B. $\frac{4}{6}$ C. $\frac{4}{4}$ D. $\frac{4}{1}$

   3.G.2

2. Which fraction is represented by the picture below?

   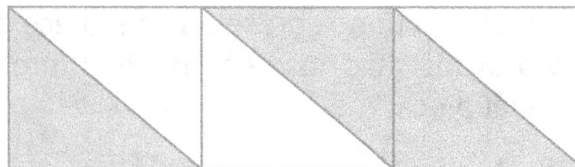

   A. $\frac{3}{3}$ B. $\frac{3}{6}$ C. $\frac{6}{3}$ D. $\frac{2}{6}$

   3.G.2

3. Jemma has divided her paper into 8 equal pieces. If she colors 6 of them black, and 1 of them brown, which fraction represents what part of her paper is colored in?

   A. $\frac{6}{8}$ B. $\frac{1}{8}$ C. $\frac{7}{8}$ D. $\frac{8}{8}$

   3.G.2

4. Which situation represents $\frac{4}{5}$?

   A. A brownie cut into 5 equal pieces, with 5 eaten
   B. A brownie cut into 5 equal pieces, with 4 eaten
   C. A brownie cut into 4 equal pieces, with 5 eaten
   D. A brownie cut into 4 equal pieces, with 4 eaten

   3.G.2

5. If Samar shaded in one more equal piece, which fraction would represent his shape?

   A. $\frac{4}{5}$ C. $\frac{5}{5}$
   B. $\frac{1}{5}$ D. $\frac{5}{1}$

   3.G.2

TIP of the DAY

The numerator helps you to know how many equal parts are selected. If your numerator is "3" as in $\frac{3}{4}$, you know that you have selected three "fourths."

130

WEEK 20 : DAY 4

1. Which picture represents a cake divided into 4 equal pieces, with one piece eaten?

   A.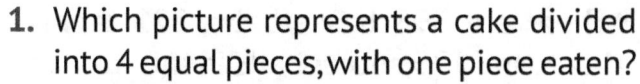
   B.
   C.
   D.

2. Which fraction represents one section of a piece of paper that has been divided into 5 equal sections.

   A. $\frac{5}{6}$ C. $\frac{4}{5}$

   B. $\frac{5}{8}$ D. $\frac{1}{5}$

3. If Julian shades in one more piece of the shape below, which fraction will represent the total shaded portion?

   A. $\frac{1}{6}$ B. $\frac{2}{6}$ C. $\frac{3}{6}$ D. $\frac{4}{6}$

4. Which fraction represents the shaded portion of a shape with 8 equal pieces, and 6 pieces shaded in?

   A. $\frac{1}{8}$ B. $\frac{6}{8}$ C. $\frac{1}{8}$ D. $\frac{2}{6}$

5. What fraction is represented by the shaded portion of the picture below?

   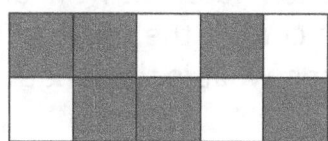

   A. $\frac{4}{6}$ B. $\frac{6}{6}$ C. $\frac{6}{10}$ D. $\frac{4}{10}$

TIP of the DAY

The bigger the denominator, the smaller the piece. For example, if you shared a cake with 10 friends $\left(\frac{1}{10}\right)$ you would have less cake than if you shared it with only 4 friends $\left(\frac{1}{4}\right)$.

131

WEEK 20 : DAY 5

ASSESSMENT

1. What fraction would represent the shaded portion if you shaded in 5 of the equal pieces below?

   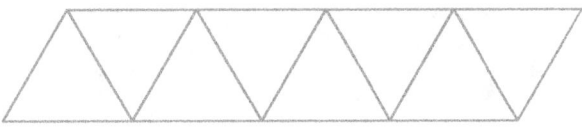

   A. $\frac{1}{8}$ B. $\frac{3}{8}$ C. $\frac{5}{8}$ D. $\frac{8}{8}$

   3.G.2

2. What would you call a quadrilateral with four equal sides and no right angles?

   A. Rhombus
   B. Square
   C. Trapezoid
   D. Rectangle

   3.G.1

3. The kitchen table has an area of 72 square inches. If the width of the table is 8 inches, what is the length?

   A. 6 inches
   B. 7 inches
   C. 8 inches
   D. 9 inches

   3.MD.7 / 3.OA.7

4. There are 398 basketballs, 221 tennis balls, and 179 soccer balls in the storage closet. *About* how many balls are there altogether in the closet, rounded to the nearest 10?

   A. 780   C. 798
   B. 790   D. 800

   3.NBT.1 / 3.NBT.2

5. Harriet has 5 boxes of fruit. Each box has 3 oranges and 6 apples. How many pieces of fruit does Harriet have altogether?

   A. 54 pieces of fruit
   B. 45 pieces of fruit
   C. 30 pieces of fruit
   D. 18 pieces of fruit

   3.OA.8

6. The shaded portion below represents how much cake Jayson has left. If he eats one more piece of cake, which fraction will represent how much cake he has left?

   A. $\frac{1}{6}$ B. $\frac{2}{6}$ C. $\frac{3}{6}$ D. $\frac{4}{6}$

   3.G.2

DAY 6 Challenge question

Yenz has a square cake. He cuts the cake into two equal pieces. Then he cuts each of those pieces into two equal pieces. Now, what fraction represents one of his equal pieces?

3.G.2

132

Great job finishing all 20 weeks! You should be ready for any test.

ASSESSMENT

VIDEO EXPLANATIONS — ARGOPREP.COM

Try this assessment to see how much you've learned - good luck!

ASSESSMENT

Question Percentage by Standard:
3.OA - 16 questions
3.NBT - 6 questions
3.NF - 10 questions
3.MD - 11 questions
3.G - 7 questions

1. Which equation represents the picture below?

   A. 5 × 6 = 5 + 5 + 5 + 5 + 5
   B. 5 × 6 = 6 + 6 + 6 + 6 + 6
   C. 5 × 6 = 5 + 5 + 6 + 6
   D. 5 × 6 = 6 + 6 + 6 + 6

   3.OA.1

2. Lilla had 345 sea shells. She sold 129 of them at the market on Saturday, and then lost 40 on the way home. How many shells does she have left?

   A. 216 shells
   B. 186 shells
   C. 177 shells
   D. 176 shells

   3.NBT.2

3. If the number line is divided into equal parts, what is the distance between O and P?

   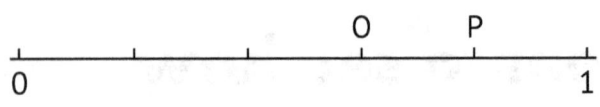

   A. $\frac{4}{5}$ B. $\frac{3}{5}$ C. $\frac{2}{5}$ D. $\frac{1}{5}$

   3.NF.2

4. Six students from Mr. Smith's class are on the playground. One-half of the students are playing on the slide. Which picture represents how many students are playing on the slide?

   A.
   B.
   C.
   D.

   3.NF.3a

5. Which situation could be represented by 2 × 8 = 16?

   A. 2 boxes with 8 cookies in each
   B. 2 boxes with 16 cookies in each
   C. 2 cookies shared between 16 boxes
   D. 8 cookies shared between 16 boxes

   3.OA.1

6. What is the quotient of 27 divided by 3?

   A. 6
   B. 7
   C. 8
   D. 9

   3.OA.2

136

ASSESSMENT

7. Which of the following numbers rounds to 400?

    A. 341
    B. 339
    C. 439
    D. 451

    3.NBT.1

8. Mr. Hill has planted flowers in his garden. The shaded portions show where he has already planted flowers. Which fraction represents how much more of the garden Mr. Hill needs to plant?

    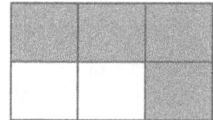

    A. $\frac{2}{4}$
    B. $\frac{2}{6}$
    C. $\frac{4}{6}$
    D. $\frac{1}{6}$

    3.NF.1

9. Which of the following expressions is equal to $\frac{3}{6}$?

    A. $\frac{1}{2} + \frac{1}{2} + \frac{1}{2}$
    B. $\frac{1}{6} + \frac{1}{6}$
    C. $\frac{3}{6} + \frac{1}{6}$
    D. $\frac{1}{6} + \frac{1}{6} + \frac{1}{6}$

    3.NF.1

10. Theo has four boxes of old books.

    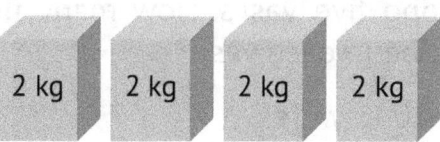

    How many **grams** do his books weigh altogether?

    A. 8,000 grams   C. 80 grams
    B. 800 grams   D. 8 grams

    3.MD.2

11. What is the area of a square with a width of 9 cm?

    A. 18 square cm
    B. 27 square cm
    C. 72 square cm
    D. 81 square cm

    3.MD.6 / 3.MD.7

12. Mason wants to cover part of his wall with the poster below.

    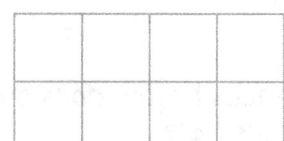 

    Mason's Wall   Mason's Poster

    Which fraction below shows the portion of Mason's wall that will be covered?

    A. $\frac{2}{2}$ C. $\frac{2}{8}$
    B. $\frac{1}{8}$ D. $\frac{6}{8}$

    3.G.2

ASSESSMENT

13. Tony has 45 flowers to divide equally among five vases. How many flowers will be in each vase?

    A. 10 flowers
    B. 9 flowers
    C. 8 flowers
    D. 7 flowers

    3.OA.2

14. Kelsey and Mary were selling bags of brownies, with 9 brownies in each bag. Kelsey sold 3 bags and Mary sold 5 bags. How many brownies did they sell altogether?

    A. 27 brownies
    B. 45 brownies
    C. 54 brownies
    D. 72 brownies

    3.OA.8

15. Which of the sequences below *does not* follow the pattern "add 4"?

    A. 3, 7, 11, 15
    B. 1, 5, 9, 13
    C. 2, 6, 11, 15
    D. 4, 8, 12, 16

    3.OA.9

16. The Third Grade has a goal to sell 650 raffle tickets. If they've already sold 479 tickets, how many more tickets do they need to sell to reach their goal?

    A. 171 tickets
    B. 181 tickets
    C. 229 tickets
    D. 271 tickets

    3.NBT.2

17. Jenna placed $\frac{3}{6}$ on a number line. What is another way to name the fraction at that location?

    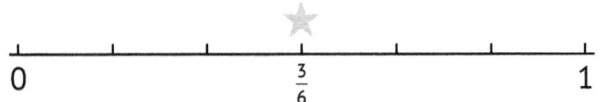

    A. $\frac{1}{6}$
    B. $\frac{1}{2}$
    C. $\frac{2}{3}$
    D. $\frac{1}{3}$

    3.NF.3a

18. James has a piece of paper that has four sides, two sets of parallel sides, and no right angles. What shape is his piece of paper?

    A. Trapezoid
    B. Square
    C. Rectangle
    D. Rhombus

    3.G.1

ASSESSMENT

19. Kylan is making a frame that will be 5 inches in length. The width will be twice as long as the length. What will be the total area of her frame?

   A. 10 square inches
   B. 25 square inches
   C. 50 square inches
   D. 55 square inches

   3.MD.5

20. Jefferson arrived at the airport at 6:45pm. If it took him 2 hours and 15 minutes to drive there, what time did he leave for the airport?

   A. 4:30pm
   B. 5:30pm
   C. 4:45pm
   D. 5:45pm

   3.MD.1

21. What name would you *not* use to describe the shape below?

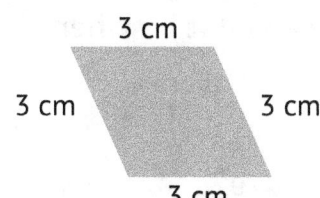

   A. Rhombus
   B. Quadrilateral
   C. Square
   D. Parallelogram

   3.G.1

22. The total perimeter around a rectangular swimming pool is 40 feet. If the width of the pool is 14 feet, what is the length?

   A. 6 feet
   B. 7 feet
   C. 8 feet
   D. 9 feet

   3.MD.8

23. Which of the following numbers *would not* round to 80?

   A. 76
   B. 81
   C. 79
   D. 85

   3.NBT.1

24. Which fraction represents the *unshaded* portion of the shape below?

   A. $\frac{2}{4}$ C. $\frac{4}{6}$
   B. $\frac{2}{6}$ D. $\frac{1}{6}$

   3.G.2

ASSESSMENT

25. The table below shows how many festival tickets were sold this week.

Day of the week	Tickets Sold
Tuesday	1
Wednesday	3
Thursday	9
Friday	27

Which pattern **best** describes the festival ticket sales?

A. Each day 2 more tickets are sold than the day before
B. Each day 6 more tickets are sold than the day before
C. Each day twice as many tickets are sold as the day before
D. Each day three times as many tickets are sold as the day before

3.OA.9

26. Nellie has 60 books in each of the boxes below. How many books does she have in all?

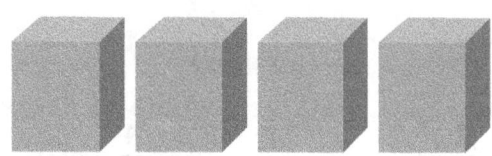

A. 180 books
B. 200 books
C. 240 books
D. 260 books

3.NBT.3

27. Which of the following statements is false?

A. $\frac{3}{6} < \frac{4}{6}$ C. $\frac{2}{3} > \frac{2}{8}$

B. $\frac{1}{2} < \frac{1}{6}$ D. $\frac{3}{3} = \frac{4}{4}$

3.NF.3

28. Which of the following amounts completes the equation?

8 kilograms = ☐ grams

A. 8
B. 80
C. 800
D. 8,000

3.MD.2

29. The time now is represented by the clock below. If Jasmyn is leaving for the movies in 2 hours and 25 minutes, what time will it be when she leaves?

A. 2:55   C. 1:45
B. 1:55   D. 2:45

3.MD.1

140

ASSESSMENT

30. Mr. Guerrero's garden has an area of 42 square feet. If the width of his garden is 6 feet, what is the length?

6 feet

?

- **A.** 5 feet
- **B.** 6 feet
- **C.** 7 feet
- **D.** 8 feet

3.MD.6 / 3.MD.7

31. What is *twice* the sum of 123 and 89?

- **A.** 424
- **B.** 246
- **C.** 212
- **D.** 202

3.OA.8

32. Max has two boxes of marbles. Each box has yellow, green, blue, red, and purple marbles in it. There are 3 of each type of marble in both boxes. How many marbles does he have in all?

- **A.** 35 marbles
- **B.** 30 marbles
- **C.** 20 marbles
- **D.** 15 marbles

3.OA.8

33. The shaded portion below represents how much cake Nelson has left. If he eats two more pieces, what fraction of the cake will be left?

- **A.** $\dfrac{3}{4}$
- **B.** $\dfrac{3}{8}$
- **C.** $\dfrac{5}{8}$
- **D.** $\dfrac{4}{8}$

3.NF.1

34. Which point represents $\dfrac{3}{4}$ on the number line below?

- **A.** P
- **B.** Q
- **C.** R
- **D.** S

3.NF.2

35. The gym teacher has 3 boxes of basketballs with 6 basketballs in each. He also has 4 boxes of tennis balls with 10 tennis balls in each. How many sport balls does he have altogether?

- **A.** 18
- **B.** 40
- **C.** 48
- **D.** 58

3.OA.8

141

ASSESSMENT

Use the following line plot to answer Questions 36 and 37.

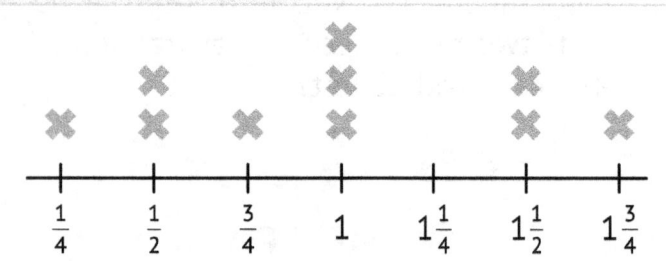

Length of Flower Stems (in Inches)

36. How many flowers had a *length less than or equal to* 1 inch?

A. 7
B. 6
C. 5
D. 4

3.MD.3 / 3.MD.4

37. Based on the line plot, how many total flowers were measured?

A. 8
B. 9
C. 10
D. 11

3.MD.3 / 3.MD.4

38. What is the name of the polygon below?

A. Rhombus
B. Square
C. Rectangle
D. Parallelogram

3.G.1

39. Which number would fill in the missing number in the equation below?

$$3 = \boxed{} \div 7$$

A. 28
B. 21
C. 14
D. 10

3.OA.3

40. Farmer Macon has 63 corn crops to plant. If he divides them equally among 7 rows, how many corn crops will be on each row?

A. 5 crops
B. 6 crops
C. 9 crops
D. 8 crops

3.OA.3

41. Which shape below represents the fraction located at the star on the number line?

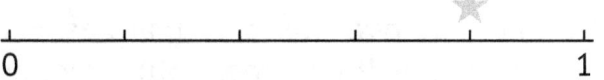

A.
B.
C.
D.

3.NF.2

142

ASSESSMENT

42. Which **two** equations could represent the array below?

- A. 5 × 3 = 15 and 5 ÷ 3 = 15
- B. 3 × 5 = 15 and 15 ÷ 5 = 3
- C. 5 × 3 = 15 and 3 ÷ 5 = 15
- D. 3 × 5 = 15 and 15 ÷ 3 = 3

3.OA.4

43. Which situation could be represented by 3 × 4 = 4 × 3?

- A. 3 bags with 4 cookies or 4 bags with 3 cookies
- B. 3 bags with 3 cookies or 4 bags with 4 cookies
- C. 4 bags with 3 cookies plus 3 more cookies
- D. 3 bags with 4 cookies plus 4 more cookies

3.OA.5

44. Marnie has 254 red beads and 578 blue beads. **About** how many beads does she have altogether, rounded to the nearest 10?

- A. 800
- B. 832
- C. 830
- D. 840

3.NBT.1 / 3.NBT.2

45. Which of the following equations **could not** represent the picture below?

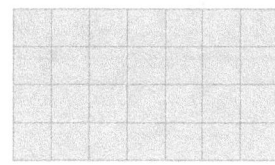

- A. 7 × 4 = 28
- B. 4 × 7 = 28
- C. 28 ÷ 7 = 4
- D. 7 ÷ 28 = 4

3.OA.6

46. Janice has a rectangle that is divided into 6 equal parts, with 4 shaded in. Which shape below **would not** represent her rectangle?

- A.
- B.
- C.
- D.

3.G.2

47. Which of the following equations is **false**?

- A. 4 × 5 = 5 × 4
- B. 3 + 6 = 6 × 3
- C. 8 + 8 = 2 × 8
- D. 6 × 7 = 7 × 6

3.OA.5

143

ASSESSMENT

48. Which fraction is represented by the star on the number line?

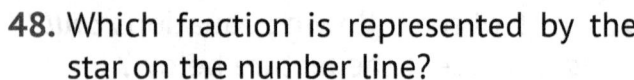

A. $\dfrac{1}{6}$ C. $\dfrac{6}{6}$

B. $\dfrac{3}{6}$ D. $\dfrac{7}{6}$

3.NF.3

50. If a polygon has 6 equal sides that are all 8 inches long, what is the total perimeter?

A. 42 inches
B. 48 inches
C. 54 inches
D. 60 inches

3.MD.8

49. If three of the equal pieces below are shaded in, which fraction will represent the portion that is *not shaded*?

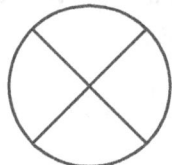

A. $\dfrac{1}{4}$ C. $\dfrac{3}{4}$

B. $\dfrac{2}{4}$ D. $\dfrac{4}{4}$

3.G.2

144

ANSWER KEY

VIDEO EXPLANATIONS

ARGOPREP.COM

ANSWER KEY

WEEK 1

DAY 1	DAY 2	DAY 3	DAY 4	DAY 5
1. B	1. C	1. D	1. B	1. D
2. D	2. D	2. B	2. A	2. C
3. C	3. C	3. C	3. A	3. D
4. D	4. A	4. B	4. C	4. C
5. A	5. C	5. D	5. B	5. B
	6. C	6. D	6. D	6. B

WEEK 2

DAY 1	DAY 2	DAY 3	DAY 4	DAY 5
1. B	1. B	1. D	1. D	1. A
2. D	2. D	2. B	2. A	2. D
3. A	3. B	3. A	3. C	3. C
4. C	4. C	4. C	4. B	4. B
5. C	5. D	5. B	5. C	5. D
	6. A			6. C

WEEK 3

DAY 1	DAY 2	DAY 3	DAY 4	DAY 5
1. A	1. A	1. D	1. C	1. B
2. D	2. D	2. B	2. D	2. D
3. C	3. C	3. D	3. A	3. C
4. C	4. C	4. C	4. B	4. C
5. B	5. B	5. B	5. C	5. B
6. D				6. D

WEEK 4

DAY 1	DAY 2	DAY 3	DAY 4	DAY 5
1. D	1. C	1. D	1. D	1. D
2. A	2. B	2. C	2. B	2. A
3. C	3. C	3. A	3. B	3. D
4. B	4. D	4. B	4. B	4. B
5. D	5. C	5. C	5. B	5. C
	6. B	6. D	6. D	6. B

WEEK 5

DAY 1	DAY 2	DAY 3	DAY 4	DAY 5
1. C	1. B	1. C	1. D	1. C
2. B	2. A	2. D	2. B	2. B
3. D	3. B	3. A	3. D	3. B
4. C	4. C	4. D	4. C	4. C
5. A	5. D	5. C	5. C	5. D
6. D	6. B	6. B	6. B	6. D

WEEK 6

DAY 1	DAY 2	DAY 3	DAY 4	DAY 5
1. B	1. D	1. C	1. C	1. B
2. D	2. C	2. D	2. D	2. A
3. A	3. D	3. B	3. B	3. C
4. D	4. C	4. C	4. D	4. B
5. B	5. B	5. A	5. A	5. D
6. D	6. A	6. B		6. B

WEEK 7

DAY 1	DAY 2	DAY 3	DAY 4	DAY 5
1. B	1. D	1. C	1. C	1. C
2. C	2. A	2. B	2. D	2. D
3. D	3. D	3. D	3. C	3. B
4. D	4. B	4. B	4. B	4. B
5. C	5. B	5. C	5. C	5. D
6. A	6. C	6. B	6. A	6. B

WEEK 8

DAY 1	DAY 2	DAY 3	DAY 4	DAY 5
1. A	1. B	1. B	1. C	1. C
2. D	2. D	2. C	2. D	2. D
3. B	3. B	3. D	3. A	3. B
4. C	4. C	4. C	4. B	4. D
5. D	5. A	5. A	5. C	5. C
6. A		6. A	6. D	6. B

ANSWER KEY

WEEK 9

DAY 1	DAY 2	DAY 3	DAY 4	DAY 5
1. C	1. C	1. B	1. D	1. B
2. B	2. A	2. D	2. C	2. B
3. C	3. B	3. C	3. B	3. D
4. D	4. D	4. B	4. A	4. C
5. B	5. B	5. D	5. C	5. C
		6. B		6. B

WEEK 10

DAY 1	DAY 2	DAY 3	DAY 4	DAY 5
1. B	1. B	1. D	1. B	1. C
2. D	2. A	2. B	2. A	2. D
3. C	3. C	3. A	3. B	3. C
4. B	4. B	4. C	4. D	4. C
5. A	5. C	5. C	5. C	5. B
6. D	6. D		6. C	6. A

WEEK 11

DAY 1	DAY 2	DAY 3	DAY 4	DAY 5
1. A	1. B	1. C	1. C	1. D
2. B	2. B	2. A	2. B	2. C
3. C	3. B	3. C	3. C	3. C
4. D	4. C	4. D	4. D	4. A
5. B	5. D	5. A	5. A	5. B
	6. A	6. B	6. B	6. D

WEEK 12

DAY 1	DAY 2	DAY 3	DAY 4	DAY 5
1. A	1. C	1. D	1. A	1. B
2. B	2. A	2. C	2. C	2. C
3. C	3. D	3. A	3. B	3. D
4. D	4. B	4. D	4. D	4. D
5. D	5. C	5. C	5. D	5. C
		6. D	6. C	6. C

WEEK 13

DAY 1	DAY 2	DAY 3	DAY 4	DAY 5
1. B	1. A	1. D	1. B	1. B
2. D	2. D	2. D	2. D	2. D
3. B	3. B	3. D	3. C	3. C
4. D	4. C	4. B	4. A	4. D
5. A	5. B	5. A	5. B	5. A
6. C	6. D	6. C	6. A	6. C

WEEK 14

DAY 1	DAY 2	DAY 3	DAY 4	DAY 5
1. D	1. C	1. D	1. A	1. D
2. B	2. A	2. C	2. C	2. C
3. C	3. C	3. B	3. B	3. A
4. C	4. B	4. A	4. C	4. D
5. B	5. C	5. D	5. D	5. D
6. D	6. C			6. B

WEEK 15

DAY 1	DAY 2	DAY 3	DAY 4	DAY 5
1. D	1. D	1. A	1. B	1. C
2. C	2. B	2. D	2. B	2. B
3. A	3. C	3. B	3. D	3. C
4. B	4. A	4. B	4. B	4. C
5. C	5. C	5. A	5. C	5. D

WEEK 16

DAY 1	DAY 2	DAY 3	DAY 4	DAY 5
1. C	1. B	1. B	1. D	1. B
2. D	2. D	2. C	2. D	2. C
3. C	3. B	3. B	3. A	3. D
4. A	4. D	4. B	4. B	4. C
5. D	5. A	5. A	5. B	5. D
6. C	6. B	6. C	6. C	6. B
7. D				

ANSWER KEY

WEEK 17

DAY 1	DAY 2	DAY 3	DAY 4	DAY 5
1. D	1. D	1. B	1. A	1. D
2. C	2. C	2. C	2. C	2. D
3. B	3. C	3. B	3. B	3. C
4. C	4. D	4. C	4. D	4. A
5. A	5. B	5. A	5. B	5. B
6. C	6. C		6. A	6. A

WEEK 18

DAY 1	DAY 2	DAY 3	DAY 4	DAY 5
1. C	1. A	1. B	1. C	1. B
2. B	2. C	2. B	2. D	2. A
3. C	3. D	3. A	3. A	3. B
4. A	4. C	4. D	4. B	4. C
5. C	5. A	5. C	5. B	5. C
	6. C	6. A		6. D

WEEK 19

DAY 1	DAY 2	DAY 3	DAY 4	DAY 5
1. D	1. C	1. C	1. C	1. A
2. D	2. B	2. A	2. D	2. B
3. D	3. C	3. D	3. C	3. C
4. C	4. D	4. B	4. D	4. B
5. B	5. A	5. C	5. C	5. B
	6. B		6. C	6. D

WEEK 20

DAY 1	DAY 2	DAY 3	DAY 4	DAY 5
1. D	1. A	1. C	1. C	1. C
2. B	2. C	2. B	2. D	2. A
3. A	3. B	3. C	3. D	3. D
4. C	4. D	4. B	4. B	4. D
5. C	5. B	5. C	5. C	5. B
				6. C

Challenge Question

Week 1: 200 + 200 + 300 = Chanel had about 700 beads.
Week 2: 343 + 459 = 802 → 802 - 219 = 583.
Week 3: 3 + 5 = 8 pieces in each bag → 8 × 9 = 72 pieces of candy total. **Week 4:** 6 × 4 = 24 pieces of candy → 24 ÷ 2 = 12 friends. **Week 5:** 3 × 12 = 36 → 36 ÷ 6 = 6 donuts on each plate. **Week 6:** (9 + 7 + 5) × 2 = 42 balls → About 40 balls. **Week 7:** (6 + 6) × 12 = 12 × 12 = 144 practices in the year. **Week 8:** 249 + 249 = 498 tokens. **Week 9:** $\frac{3}{8} + \frac{2}{8} = \frac{5}{8}$ of the pie. **Week 10:** $\frac{2}{8} + \frac{3}{8} = \frac{5}{8}$ → $\frac{8}{8} - \frac{5}{8} = \frac{3}{8}$ of the marathon left. **Week 11:** Jack ate more because $\frac{3}{5}$ is larger than $\frac{2}{4}$. **Week 12:** 1:30pm + 45 = 2:15pm → 2:15pm + 35 = 2:50pm → 2:50pm + 1 hour = 3:50pm. **Week 13:** 3 + 3 = 6 liters of juice → 6 liters + 3 liters = 9 liters = 9,000 milliliters of juice. **Week 14:** 7:30pm - 3 hours = 4:30pm → 4:30pm - 25 minutes = 4:05pm. **Week 15:** 4 and $\frac{1}{4}$ inches, 4 and $\frac{1}{2}$ inches, and 4 and $\frac{3}{4}$ inches. **Week 16:** Callie's Sandbox = 4 × 5 = 20 feet squared → Hannah's sandbox = 20 × 2 = 40 feet squared. **Week 17:** Classroom area = 12 × 12 = 144 feet squared → Carpet area = 4 × 9 = 36 square feet → Classroom floor without carpet = 144 - 36 = 108 square feet. **Week 18:** 3 inches and 8 inches; 2 inches and 12 inches; 4 inches and 6 inches. **Week 19:** Square = 12 + 12 + 12 + 12 = 48 inches → Rhombus = 12 + 12 + 12 + 12 = 48 inches → 48 + 48 = 96 inches. **Week 20:** Cut in two: $\frac{1}{2}$ → cut in two: $\frac{1}{4}$. Each piece is $\frac{1}{4}$.

Assessment

1. B	11. D	21. C	31. A	41. A
2. D	12. C	22. A	32. B	42. B
3. D	13. B	23. D	33. B	43. A
4. B	14. D	24. B	34. C	44. C
5. A	15. C	25. D	35. D	45. D
6. D	16. A	26. C	36. A	46. C
7. C	17. B	27. B	37. C	47. B
8. B	18. D	28. D	38. D	48. C
9. D	19. C	29. A	39. B	49. A
10. A	20. A	30. C	40. C	50. B

SOCIAL STUDIES

Social Studies Daily Practice Workbook by ArgoPrep allows students to build foundational skills and review concepts. Our workbooks explore social studies topics in depth with ArgoPrep's 5 E's to build social studies mastery.

Want free K-8 **math** and *English* worksheets?
Visit us at:
argoprep.com/worksheets

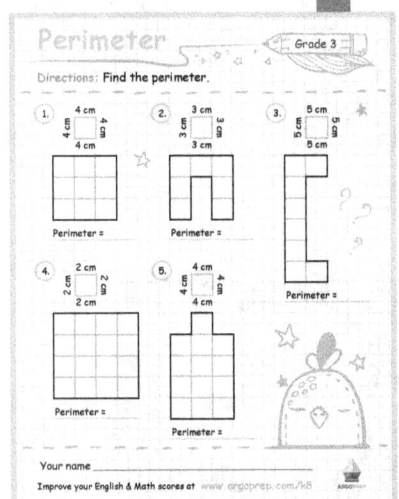

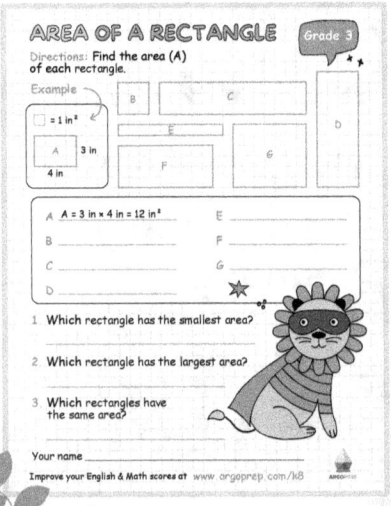

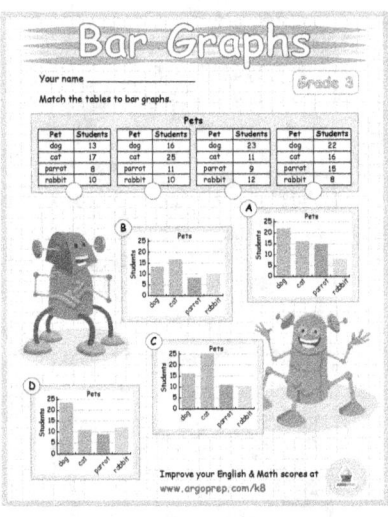

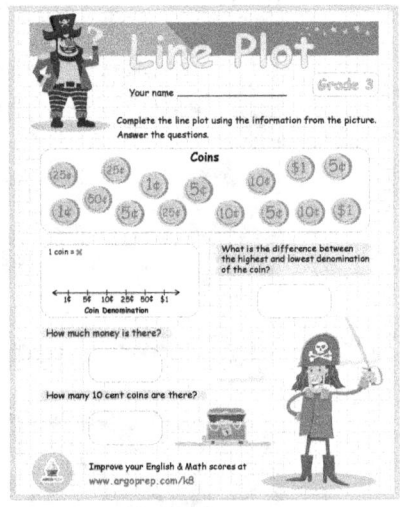

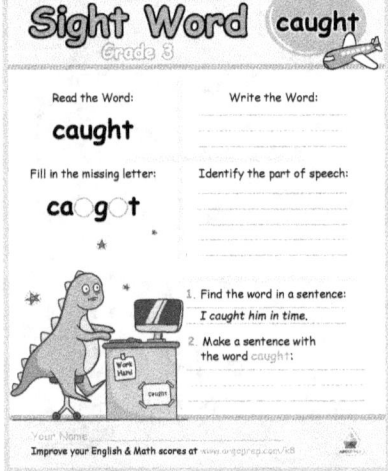

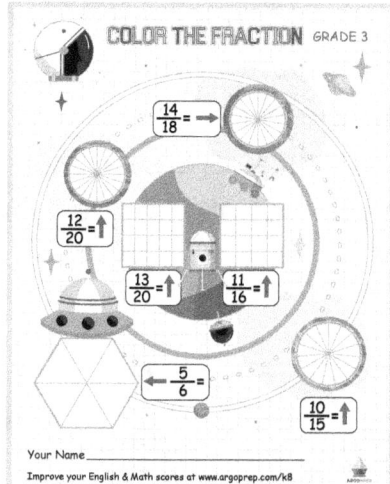
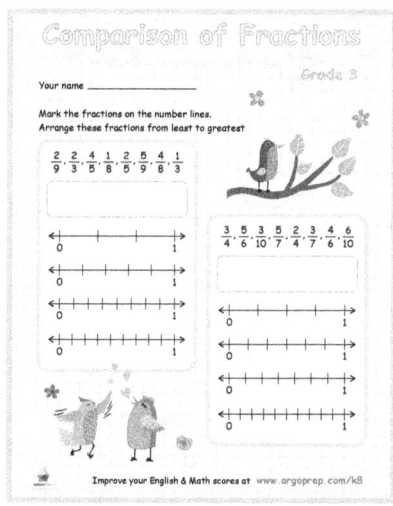

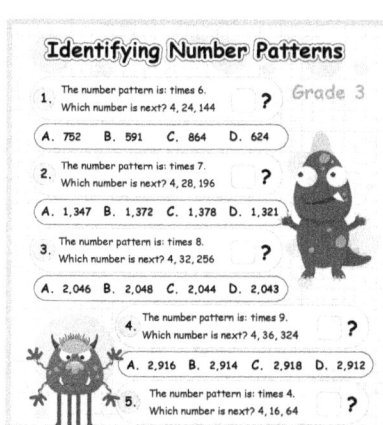
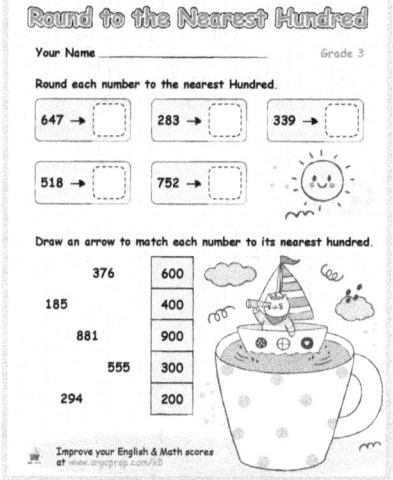

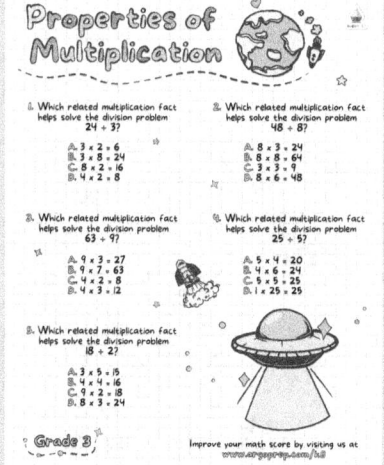
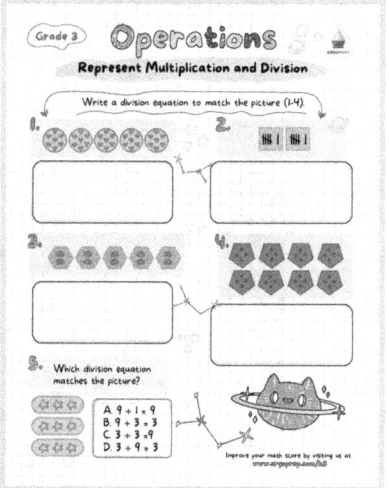

KIDS WINTER ACADEMY

Kids Winter Academy by ArgoPrep covers material learned in September through December so your child can reinforce the concepts they should have learned in class. We recommend using this particular series during the winter break. These workbooks include two weeks of activities for math, reading, science, and social studies. Best of all, you can access detailed video explanations to all the questions on our website.

argoprep.com

DIPLOMA

The certificate is presented to:

_____
your name

_____
by school name

for successful completion of ArgoPrep's Grade 3 workbook
Excellent work!

_____   _____
Date   *Signature*

3rd Grade